STORIES FROM LE MORTE D'ARTHUR AND THE MABINOGION

BEATRICE E. CLAY

Double 9 BOOKS

Stories From Le Morte D'arthur And The Mabinogion
by Beatrice E. Clay

ISBN: 978-93-59396-22-4

Published by

DOUBLE 9 BOOKS

2/13-B, Ansari Road, Daryaganj
New Delhi – 110002
info@double9books.com
www.double9books.com
Tel. 011-40042856

ABOUT THE AUTHOR

Beatrice E. Clay is an author known for her literary works that explore diverse themes and genres. With a talent for storytelling, she captures the imagination of readers through her engaging narratives and also compelling characters. Drawing from various sources, Beatrice E. Clay's writing exhibits a deep appreciation for mythology, folklore, and other one historical legends. Her evocative prose and attention to detail transport readers to captivating worlds, making her works a delightful escape into realms of fantasy and also adventure. Beatrice E. Clay's storytelling prowess weaves together ancient myths and timeless tales, bringing new life to classic stories and also introducing them to modern audiences. Through her works, Beatrice E. Clay showcases a passion for the art of storytelling and also a keen understanding of the human experience. Her literary contributions offer thought-provoking insights and emotional resonance, leaving a lasting impact on those who delve into her works.

CONTENTS

Introduction

Among the stories of world-wide renown, not the least stirring are those that have gathered about the names of national heroes. The *Æneid*, the *Nibelungenlied*, the *Chanson de Roland*, the *Morte D'Arthur*,—they are not history, but they have been as National Anthems to the races, and their magic is not yet dead.

In olden times our forefathers used to say that the world had seen nine great heroes, three heathen, three Jewish, and three Christian; among the Christian heroes was British Arthur, and of none is the fame greater. Even to the present day, his name lingers in many widely distant places. In the peninsula of Gower, a huge slab of rock, propped up on eleven short pillars, is still called Arthur's Stone; the lofty ridge which looks down upon Edinburgh bears the name of Arthur's Seat; and—strangest, perhaps, of all—in the Franciscan Church of far-away Innsbrück, the finest of the ten statues of ancestors guarding the tomb of the Emperor Maximilian I. is that of King Arthur. There is hardly a country in Europe without its tales of the Warrior-King; and yet of any real Arthur history tells us little, and that little describes, not the knightly conqueror, but the king of a broken people, struggling for very life.

More than fifteen centuries ago, this country, now called England, was inhabited by a Celtic race known as the Britons, a warlike people, divided into numerous tribes constantly at war with each other. But in the first century of the Christian era they were conquered by the Romans, who added Britain to their vast empire and held it against attacks from without and rebellions from within by stationing legions, or troops of soldiers, in strongly fortified places all over the country. Now, from their conquerors, the Britons learnt many useful arts, to read and to write, to build houses and to make roads; but at the same time, they unlearnt some of their own virtues and, among others, how to think and act for themselves. For the Romans never allowed a Briton any real part in the government of his own country, and if he wished to become a soldier, he was sent away from Britain to serve with a legion stationed in some far-distant part of the empire. Thus it came about that when, in the fifth century, the Romans withdrew from Britain to defend Rome itself from invading hordes of savages, the unhappy Britons had forgotten how to govern and how to defend themselves, and fell an easy prey to the many enemies waiting to pounce on their defenceless country. Picts from Scotland invaded the north, and Scots from Ireland plundered the west; worst of all, the heathen Angles and Saxons, pouring across the seas from their homes in the Elbe country, wasted the land with fire and sword. Many of the Britons were slain; those who escaped sought refuge in the mountainous parts of the west from Cornwall to the Firth of Clyde. There, forgetting, to some extent, their quarrels, they took the name of the Cymry, which means the "Brethren," though the English, unable to understand their language, spoke of them contemptuously as the "Welsh," or the "Strangers."

For a long time the struggle went on between the two races, and nowhere mere fiercely than in the south-west, where the invaders set up the Kingdom of Wessex; but at last there arose among the Britons a great chieftain called Arthur. The old histories speak of him as "Emperor," and he seems to have been obeyed by all the Britons; perhaps, therefore, he had succeeded to the position of the Roman official known as the Comes Britanniæ, whose duty it was to hasten to the aid of the local governors in defending any part of Britain where danger threatened. At all events, under his leadership, the oppressed people defeated the Saxons in a desperate fight at Mons Badonicus, perhaps the little place in Dorsetshire known as Badbury, or, it may be, Bath itself, which is still called Badon by the Welsh. After that victory, history has little to say about Arthur. The stories tell that he was killed in a great battle in the west; but, nowadays, the wisest historians think it more probable that he met his death in a conflict near the River Forth.

And so, in history, Arthur, the hero of such a mass of romantic story, is little more than a name, and it is hardly possible to explain how he attained to such renown as the hero of marvellous and, sometimes, magical feats, unless on the supposition that he became confused with some legendary hero, half god, half man, whose fame he added to his own. Perhaps not the least marvel about him is that he who was the hero of the Britons, should have become the national hero of the English race that he spent his life in fighting. Yet that is what did happen, though not till long afterwards, when the victorious English, in their turn, bent before their conquering kinsmen, the Normans.

Now in the reign of the third Norman king, Henry I., there lived a certain Welsh priest known as Geoffrey of Monmouth. Geoffrey seems to have been much about the Court, and perhaps it was the Norman love of stories that first made him think of writing his *History of the British Kings*. A wonderful tale he told of all the British kings from the time that Brut the Trojan settled in the country and called it, after himself, Britain! For Geoffrey's book was history only in name. What he tells us is that he was given an ancient chronicle found in Brittany, and was asked to translate it from Welsh into the better known language, Latin. It is hardly likely, however, that Geoffrey himself expected his statement to be taken quite seriously. Even in his own day, not every one believed in him, for a certain Yorkshire monk declared that the historian had "lied saucily and shamelessly"; and some years later, Gerald the Welshman tells of a man who had intercourse with devils, from whose sway, however, he could be freed if a Bible were placed upon his breast, whereas he was completely under their control if Geoffrey's *History* were laid upon him, just because the book was so full of lies.

It is quite certain that Geoffrey did not write history, but he did make a capital story, partly by collecting legends about British heroes, partly by inventing stories of his own; so that though he is not entitled to fame as an historian, he may claim to rank high as a romantic story-teller who set a fashion destined to last for some three centuries.

So popular was his book that, not only in England, but, in an even greater degree, on the Continent, writers were soon at work, collecting and making more stories about the greatest of his kings, Arthur. By some it is thought that the Normans took such delight in the knightly deeds of Geoffrey's heroes that they spread the story in France when they visited their homes in Normandy. Moreover, they were in a good position to learn other tales of their favourite knights, for Normandy bordered on Brittany, the home of the Bretons, who, being of the same race as the Welsh, honoured the same heroes in their legends. So in return for Geoffrey's tales, Breton stories, perhaps, found their way into England; at all events, marvellous romances of King Arthur and his Round Table were soon being told in England, in France, in Germany and in Italy.

Now, to some it may seem strange that story-tellers should care to weave their stories so constantly about the same personages; strange, too, that they should invent stories about men and women who were believed actually to have existed. But it must be remembered that, in those early days, very few could read and write, and that, before printing was invented, books were so scarce that four or five constituted quite a library. Those who knew how to read, and were so fortunate as to have books, read them again and again. For the rest, though kings and great nobles might have poets attached to their courts, the majority depended for their amusement on the professional story-teller. In the long winter evening, no one was more welcome than the wandering minstrel. He might be the knightly troubadour who, accompanied by a jongleur to play his accompaniments, wandered from place to place out of sheer love of his art and of adventure; more often, however, the minstrel made story-telling his trade, and gained his living from the bounty of his audience—be it in castle, market-place, or inn. Most commonly, the narratives took the form of long rhyming poems; not because the people in those days were so poetical—indeed, some of these poems would be thought, in present times, very dreary doggerel—but because rhyme is easier to remember than prose. Story-tellers had generally much the same stock-in-trade—stories of Arthur, Charlemagne, Sir Guy of Warwick, Sir Bevis of Southampton, and so on. If a minstrel had skill of his own, he would invent some new episode, and so, perhaps, turn a compliment to his patron by introducing the exploit of an ancestor, at the same time that he made his story last longer. People did not weary of hearing the same tales over and over again, any more than little children get tired of nursery rhymes, or their elders turn away from "Punch and Judy," though the same little play has been performed for centuries. As for inventing stories about real people, that may well have seemed permissible in an age when historians recorded mere hearsay as actual fact. Richard III., perhaps, had one shoulder higher than the other, but within a few years of his death grave historians had represented him as a hunchbacked deformity.

The romances connected with King Arthur and his knights went on steadily growing in number until the fifteenth century; of them, some have survived to the present day, but undoubtedly many have been lost. Then, in the latter half of the fifteenth century, the most famous of all the Arthurian stories was given to the world in Sir Thomas Malory's *Morte D'Arthur*. By good luck, the great printer who made it one of his first works, has left an account of the circumstances that led to its production. In the reign of Edward IV., William Caxton set up his printing-press (the first in England) in the precincts of Westminster Abbey. There he was visited, as he himself relates, by "many noble and divers gentlemen" demanding why he had not printed the "noble history of the Saint Grail and of the most-renowned Christian King ... Arthur." To please them, and because he himself loved chivalry, Caxton printed Sir Thomas Malory's story, in which all that is best in the many Arthurian romances is woven into one grand narrative.

Since then, in our own days, the story of Arthur and his knights has been told in beautiful verse by Lord Tennyson; but for the originals of some of his poems it would be useless to look in Malory. The story of Geraint and Enid, Tennyson derived from a very interesting collection of translations of ancient Welsh stories made by Lady Charlotte Guest, and by her called *Mabinogion*,[1] although not all Welsh scholars would consider the name quite accurate.

[1] Meaning the apprentices of the bards.

And now it is time to say something about the stories themselves. The Arthur of history was engaged in a life-long struggle with an enemy that threatened to rob his people of home, of country, and of freedom; in the stories, the king and his knights, like Richard Coeur-de-Lion, sought adventure for adventure's sake, or, as in the case of Sir Peredur, took fantastic vows for the love of a lady. The Knights of the Round Table are sheathed from head to foot in plate armour, although the real Arthur's warriors probably had only shirts of mail and shields with which to ward off the blows of the enemy. They live in moated castles instead of in halls of wood, and they are more often engaged in tournaments than in struggles with the heathen. In fact, those who wrote the stories represented their heroes as living such lives as they themselves led. Just in the same way, Dutch painters used to represent the shepherds in the Bible story as Dutch peasants; just so David Garrick, the great actor of the eighteenth century, used to act the part of a Roman in his own full-bottomed wig and wide-skirted coat.

It must not be forgotten that, in those far-away days when there were few who could even read or write, there was little that, in their ignorance, people were not prepared to believe. Stories of marvels and magic that would deceive no one now, were then eagerly accepted as truth. Those were the days when philosophers expected to discover the Elixir of Life; when doctors consulted the stars in treating their patients; when a noble of the royal blood, such as Humphrey, Duke of Gloucester, could fall into disgrace because his wife was accused of trying to compass the king's death by melting a wax image of him before a slow fire.

Of all the stories, perhaps the most mystical is that of the Quest of the Holy Grail, and it has features peculiar to itself. Nuns take the place of fair ladies; there are hermitages instead of castles; and the knights themselves, if they do not die, become monks or hermits. The reason for this change in scene and character is, that this is a romance in which the Church was trying to teach men, by means of a tale such as they loved, the lesson of devotion and purity of heart.

The story sprang from certain legends which had grown up about the name of Joseph of Arimathea. It was related that, when our Lord was crucified, Joseph caught in a dish, or vessel, the blood which flowed from His wounded side. In later years, the pious Jew left his home and, taking with him the precious vessel, sailed away on unknown seas until he came to the land of Britain. In that country he landed, and at Glastonbury he built himself a hermitage, where he treasured the sacred dish which came to be known as the Saint Grail. After Joseph's death, the world grew more wicked, and so the Holy Grail disappeared from the sight of sinful men, although, from time to time, the vision of it was granted, as in the story, to the pure in heart.

In later days, legend said that where Joseph's hermitage had stood, there grew up the famous monastery of Glastonbury, and it came to have a special importance of its own in the Arthurian romance. In the reign of Henry II., by the king's orders, the monks of Glastonbury made search for the grave of King Arthur, and, in due time, they announced that they had found it, nine feet below the soil, the coffin covered with a stone in which was inlaid a leaden cross bearing this inscription: "Hic iacet sepultus inclitus rex Arthurius in insula Avalonia." Some, however, suggested that the monks, less honest than anxious to please the masterful king, had first placed the stone in position and then found it!

One more feature of the tales remains to be mentioned: their geography. There is no atlas that will make it plain in all cases; and this is hardly wonderful, for so little was known of this subject that, even in the reign of Henry VIII., the learned Lord Berners was quite satisfied that his hero should journey to Babylon by way of the Nile! Some of the places mentioned in the stories are, of course, familiar, and others, less well known, can, with a little care, be traced; but to identify all is not possible. Caerleon, where King Arthur so often held his Court, still bears the same name, though its glory has sorely shrank since the days when it had a bishop of its own. Camelot, where stood the marvellous palace built for the king by Merlin, is perhaps the village of Queen's Camel in Somersetshire. If it is borne in mind that the French call Wales *Pays de Galles*, it is not difficult to see that North Galis may well be North Wales. Gore is the peninsula of Gower; Liones probably the land south-west of Cornwall, now sunk beneath the sea; and Avalonia was the name given to one of the many small islands of the once marshy, low-lying shore of Somersetshire, which became afterwards better known as Glastonbury.

Happily, it is neither on their history nor on their geography that the tales depend for their interest. As long as a story of adventure thrills; as long as gentleness, courtesy and consideration for the weak excite respect, so long will be read the tales of the brave times

"When every morning brought a noble chance,

And every chance brought out a noble knight."

BOOK I
THE COMING OF ARTHUR

CHAPTER I
OF ARTHUR'S BIRTH; AND
HOW HE BECAME KING

Long years ago, there ruled over Britain a king called Uther Pendragon. A mighty prince was he, and feared by all men; yet, when he sought the love of the fair Igraine of Cornwall, she would have naught to do with him, so that, from grief and disappointment, Uther fell sick, and at last seemed like to die.

Now in those days, there lived a famous magician named Merlin, so powerful that he could change his form at will, or even make himself invisible; nor was there any place so remote but that he could reach it at once, merely by wishing himself there. One day, suddenly he stood at Uther's bedside, and said: "Sir King, I know thy grief, and am ready to help thee. Only promise to give me, at his birth, the son that shall be born to thee, and thou shalt have thy heart's desire." To this the king agreed joyfully, and Merlin kept his word: for he gave Uther the form of one whom Igraine had loved dearly, and so she took him willingly for her husband.

When the time had come that a child should be born to the King and Queen, Merlin appeared before Uther to remind him of his promise; and Uther swore it should be as he had said. Three days later, a prince was born, and, with pomp and ceremony, was christened by the name of Arthur; but immediately thereafter, the King commanded that the child should be carried to the postern-gate, there to be given to the old man who would be found waiting without.

Not long after, Uther fell sick, and he knew that his end was come; so, by Merlin's advice, he called together his knights and barons, and said to them: "My death draws near. I charge you, therefore, that ye obey my son even as ye have obeyed me; and my curse upon him if he claim not the crown when he is a man grown." Then the King turned his face to the wall and died.

Scarcely was Uther laid in his grave before disputes arose. Few of the nobles had seen Arthur or even heard of him, and not one of them would have been willing to be ruled by a child; rather, each thought himself fitted to be king, and, strengthening his own castle, made war on his neighbours until confusion alone was supreme, and the poor groaned because there was none to help them.

Now when Merlin carried away Arthur — for Merlin was the old man who had stood at the postern-gate — he had known all that would happen, and had taken the child to keep him safe from the fierce barons until he should be of age to rule wisely and well, and perform all the wonders prophesied of him. He gave the child to the care of the good knight Sir Ector to bring up with his son Kay, but revealed not to him that it was the son of Uther Pendragon that was given into his charge.

At last, when years had passed and Arthur was grown a tall youth well skilled in knightly exercises, Merlin went to the Archbishop of Canterbury and advised him that he should call together at Christmas-time all the chief men of the realm to the great cathedral in London; "For," said Merlin, "there shall be seen a great marvel by which it shall be made clear to all men who is the lawful King of this land." The Archbishop did as Merlin counselled. Under pain of a fearful curse, he bade barons and knights come to London to keep the feast, and to pray heaven to send peace to the realm.

The people hastened to obey the Archbishop's commands, and, from all sides, barons and knights came riding in to keep the birth-feast of our Lord. And when they had prayed, and were coming forth from the cathedral, they saw a strange sight. There, in the open space before the church, stood, on a great stone, an anvil thrust through with a sword; and on the stone were written these words: "Whoso can draw forth this sword, is rightful King of Britain born."

At once there were fierce quarrels, each man clamouring to be the first to try his fortune, none doubting his own success. Then the Archbishop decreed that each should make the venture in turn, from the greatest baron to the least knight; and each in turn, having put forth his utmost strength, failed to move the sword one inch, and drew back ashamed. So the Archbishop dismissed the company, and having appointed guards to watch over the stone, sent messengers through all the land to give word of great jousts to be held in London at Easter, when each knight could give proof of his skill and courage, and try whether the adventure of the sword was for him.

Among those who rode to London at Easter was the good Sir Ector, and with him his son, Sir Kay, newly made a knight, and the young Arthur. When the morning came that the jousts should begin, Sir Kay and Arthur mounted their horses and set out for the lists; but before they reached the field, Kay looked and saw that he had left his sword behind. Immediately Arthur turned back to fetch it for him, only to find the house fast shut, for all were gone to view the tournament. Sore vexed was Arthur, fearing lest his brother Kay should lose his chance of gaining glory, till, of a sudden, he bethought him of the sword in the great anvil before the cathedral. Thither he rode with all speed, and the guards having deserted their post to view the tournament, there was none to forbid him the adventure. He leaped from his horse, seized the hilt, and instantly drew forth the sword as easily as from a scabbard; then, mounting his horse and thinking no marvel of what he had done, he rode after his brother and handed him the weapon.

When Kay looked at it, he saw at once that it was the wondrous sword from the stone. In great joy he sought his father, and showing it to him, said: "Then must I be King of Britain." But Sir Ector bade him say how he came by the sword, and when Sir Kay told how Arthur had brought it to him, Sir Ector bent his knee to the boy, and said: "Sir, I perceive that ye are my King, and here I tender you my homage"; and Kay did as his father. Then the three sought the Archbishop, to whom they related all that had happened; and he, much marvelling, called the people together to the great stone, and bade Arthur thrust back the sword and draw it forth again in the presence of all, which he did with ease. But an angry murmur arose from the barons, who cried that what a boy could do, a man could do; so, at the Archbishop's word, the sword was put back, and each man, whether baron or knight, tried in his turn to draw it forth, and failed. Then, for the third time, Arthur drew forth the sword. Immediately there arose from the people a great shout: "Arthur is King! Arthur is King! We will have no King but Arthur"; and, though the great barons scowled and threatened, they fell on their knees before him while the Archbishop placed the crown upon his head, and swore to obey him faithfully as their lord and sovereign.

Thus Arthur was made King; and to all he did justice, righting wrongs and giving to all their dues. Nor was he forgetful of those that had been his friends; for Kay, whom he loved as a brother, he made Seneschal and chief of his household, and to Sir Ector, his foster-father, he gave broad lands.

CHAPTER II
THE ROUND TABLE

Thus Arthur was made King, but he had to fight for his own; for eleven great kings drew together and refused to acknowledge him as their lord, and chief amongst the rebels was King Lot of Orkney who had married Arthur's sister, Bellicent.

By Merlin's advice, Arthur sent for help overseas, to Ban and Bors, the two great Kings who ruled in Gaul. With their aid, he overthrew his foes in a great battle near the river Trent; and then he passed with them into their own lands and helped them drive out their enemies. So there was ever great friendship between Arthur and the Kings Ban and Bors, and all their kindred; and afterwards some of the most famous Knights of the Round Table were of that kin.

Then King Arthur set himself to restore order throughout his kingdom. To all who would submit and amend their evil ways, he showed kindness; but those who persisted in oppression and wrong he removed, putting in their places others who would deal justly with the people. And because the land had become overrun with forest during the days of misrule, he cut roads through the thickets, that no longer wild beasts and men, fiercer than the beasts, should lurk in their gloom, to the harm of the weak and defenceless. Thus it came to pass that soon the peasant ploughed his fields in safety, and where had been wastes, men dwelt again in peace and prosperity.

Amongst the lesser kings whom Arthur helped to rebuild their towns and restore order, was King Leodegrance of Cameliard. Now Leodegrance had one fair child, his daughter Guenevere; and from the time that first he saw her, Arthur gave her all his love. So he sought counsel of Merlin, his chief adviser. Merlin heard the King sorrowfully, and he said: "Sir King, when a man's heart is set, he may not change. Yet had it been well if ye had loved another."

So the King sent his knights to Leodegrance, to ask of him his daughter; and Leodegrance consented, rejoicing to wed her to so good and knightly a King. With great pomp, the princess was conducted to Canterbury, and there the King met her, and they two were wed by the Archbishop in the great Cathedral, amid the rejoicings of the people.

On that same day did Arthur found his Order of the Round Table, the fame of which was to spread throughout Christendom and endure through all time. Now the Round Table had been made for King Uther Pendragon by Merlin, who had meant thereby to set forth plainly to all men the roundness of the earth. After Uther died, King Leodegrance had possessed it; but when Arthur was wed, he sent it to him as a gift, and great was the King's joy at receiving it. One hundred and fifty knights might take their places about it, and for them Merlin made sieges or seats. One hundred and twenty-eight did Arthur knight at that great feast; thereafter, if any sieges were empty, at the high festival of Pentecost new knights were ordained to fill them, and by magic was the name of each knight found inscribed, in letters of gold, in his proper siege. One seat only long remained unoccupied, and that was the Siege Perilous. No knight might occupy it until the coming of Sir Galahad; for, without danger to his life, none might sit there who was not free from all stain of sin.

With pomp and ceremony did each knight take upon him the vows of true knighthood: to obey the King; to show mercy to all who asked it; to defend the weak; and for no worldly gain to fight in a wrongful cause: and all the knights rejoiced together, doing honour to Arthur and to his Queen. Then they rode forth to right the wrong and help the oppressed, and by their aid, the King held his realm in peace, doing justice to all.

CHAPTER III
OF THE FINDING OF EXCALIBUR

Now when Arthur was first made King, as young knights will, he courted peril for its own sake, and often would he ride unattended by lonely forest ways, seeking the adventure that chance might send him. All unmindful was he of the ruin to his realm if mischief befell him; and even his trusty counsellors, though they grieved that he should thus imperil him, yet could not but love him the more for his hardihood.

So, on a day, he rode through the Forest Perilous where dwelt the Lady Annoure, a sorceress of great might, who used her magic powers but for the furtherance of her own desires. And as she looked from a turret window, she descried King Arthur come riding down a forest glade, and the sunbeams falling upon him made one glory of his armour and of his yellow hair. Then, as Annoure gazed upon the King, her heart grew hot within her, and she resolved that, come what might, she would have him for her own, to dwell with her always and fulfil all her behests. And so she bade lower the drawbridge and raise the portcullis, and sallying forth accompanied by her maidens, she gave King Arthur courteous salutation, and prayed him that he would rest within her castle that day, for that she had a petition to make to him; and Arthur, doubting nothing of her good faith, suffered himself to be led within.

Then was a great feast spread, and Annoure caused the King to be seated in a chair of state at her right hand, while squires and pages served him on bended knee. So when they had feasted, the King turned to the Lady Annoure and said courteously: "Lady, somewhat ye said of a request that ye would make. If there be aught in which I may pleasure you, I pray you let me know it, and I will serve you as knightly as I may." "In truth," said the lady, "there is that which I would fain entreat of you, most noble knight; yet suffer, I beseech you, that first I may show you somewhat of my castle and my estate, and then will I crave a boon of your chivalry." Then the sorceress led King Arthur from room to room of her castle, and ever each displayed greater store of beauty than the last. In some the walls were hung with rich tapestries, in others they gleamed with precious stones; and the

King marvelled what might be the petition of one that was mistress of such wealth. Lastly, Annoure brought the King out upon the battlements, and as he gazed around him, he saw that, since he had entered the castle, there had sprung up about it triple walls of defence that shut out wholly the forest from view. Then turned he to Annoure, and gravely he said: "Lady, greatly I marvel in what a simple knight may pleasure one that is mistress of so wondrous a castle as ye have shown me here; yet if there be aught in which I may render you knightly service, right gladly would I hear it now, for I must forth upon my way to render service to those whose knight I am sworn." "Nay, now, King Arthur," answered the sorceress mockingly, "ye may not think to deceive me; for well I know you, and that all Britain bows to your behest." "The more reason then that I should ride forth to right wrong and succour them that, of their loyalty, render true obedience to their lord." "Ye speak as a fool," said the sorceress; "why should one that may command be at the beck and call of every hind and slave within his realm? Nay, rest thee here with me, and I will make thee ruler of a richer land than Britain, and give thee to satisfy thy every desire." "Lady," said the King sternly, "I will hear and judge of your petition at this time, and then will I forth upon my way." "Nay," said Annoure, "there needs not this harshness. I did but speak for thine advantage. Only vow thee to my service, and there is naught that thou canst desire that thou shalt not possess. Thou shalt be lord of this fair castle and of the mighty powers that obey me. Why waste thy youth in hardship and in the service of such as shall render thee little enough again?"

Thereupon, without ever a word, the King turned him about and made for the turret stair by which he had ascended, but nowhere could he find it. Then said the sorceress, mocking him: "Fair sir, how think ye to escape without my good-will? See ye not the walls that guard my stronghold? And think ye that I have not servants enow to do my bidding?" She clapped her hands and forthwith there appeared a company of squires who, at her command, seized the King and bore him away to a strong chamber where they locked him in.

And so the King abode that night, the prisoner of that evil sorceress, with little hope that day, when it dawned, should bring him better cheer. Yet lost he not courage, but kept watch and vigil the night through lest the powers of evil should assail him unawares. And with the early morning light, Annoure came to visit him. More stately she seemed than the night before, more tall and more terrible; and her dress was one blaze of flashing gems, so that scarce could the eye look upon her. As a queen might address a vassal, so greeted she the King, and as condescending to one of low estate, asked how he had fared that night. And the King made answer: "I have kept vigil as behoves a knight who, knowing him to be in the midst of danger, would bear himself meetly in any peril that should offer." And the Lady Annoure, admiring his knightly courage, desired more earnestly even than before to win him to her will, and she said: "Sir Arthur, I know well your courage and knightly fame, and greatly do I desire to keep you with me. Stay with me and I promise you that ye shall bear sway over a wider realm than any that ever ye heard of, and I, even I, its mistress, will be at your command. And what lose ye if ye accept my offer? Little enough, I ween, for never think that ye shall win the world from evil and men to loyalty and truth." Then answered the King in anger: "Full well I see that thou art in league with evil and that thou but seekest to turn me from my purpose. I defy thee, foul sorceress. Do thy worst; though thou slay me, thou shalt never sway me to thy will"; and therewith the King raised his cross-hilted sword before her. Then the lady quailed at that sight. Her heart was filled with hate, but she said: "Go your way, proud King of a petty realm. Rule well your race of miserable mortals, since more it pleasures you than to bear sway over the powers of the air. I keep you not against your will." With these words, she passed from the chamber, and the King heard her give command to her squires to set him without her gates, give him his horse, and suffer him to go on his way.

And so it came to pass that the King found himself once more at large, and marvelled to have won so lightly to liberty. Yet knew he not the depths of treachery in the heart of Annoure; for when she found she might not prevail with the King, she bethought her how, by mortal means, she might bring the King to dishonour and death. And so, by her magic art, she caused the King to follow a path that brought him to a fountain, whereby a knight had his tent, and, for love of adventure, held the way against all comers. Now this knight was Sir Pellinore, and at that time he had not his equal for strength and knightly skill, nor had any been found that might stand against him. So, as the King drew nigh, Pellinore cried: "Stay, knight, for none passes this way except he joust with me." "That is no good custom," said the King; "it were well that ye followed it no more." "It is my custom, and I will follow it still," answered Pellinore; "if ye like it not, amend it if ye may." "I will do my endeavour," said Arthur, "but, as ye see, I have no spear." "Nay, I seek not to have you at advantage," replied Pellinore, and bade his squire give Arthur a spear. Then they dressed their shields, laid their lances in rest, and rushed upon each other. Now the King was wearied by his night's vigil, and the strength of Pellinore was as the strength of three men; so, at the first encounter, Arthur was unhorsed. Then said he: "I have lost the honour on horseback, but now will I encounter thee with my sword and on foot." "I, too, will alight," said Pellinore; "small honour to me were it if I slew thee on foot, I being horsed the while." So they encountered each other on foot, and so fiercely they fought that they hewed off great pieces of each other's armour and the ground was dyed with their blood. But at the last, Arthur's sword broke off short at the hilt, and so he stood all defenceless before his foe. "I have thee now," cried Pellinore; "yield thee as recreant or I will slay thee." "That will I never," said the King, "slay me if thou canst." Then he sprang on Pellinore, caught him by the middle, and flung him to the ground, himself falling with him. And Sir Pellinore marvelled, for never before had he encountered so bold and resolute a foe; but exerting his great strength, he rolled himself over, and so brought Arthur beneath him. Then had Arthur perished, but at that moment Merlin stood beside him, and when Sir Pellinore would have struck off the King's head, stayed his blow, crying: "Pellinore, if thou slayest this knight, thou puttest the whole realm in peril; for this is none other than King Arthur himself." Then was Pellinore filled with dread, and cried: "Better make an end of him at once; for if I suffer him to live, what hope have I of his grace, that have dealt with him so sorely?" But before Pellinore could strike, Merlin caused a deep sleep to come upon him; and raising King Arthur from the ground, he staunched his wounds and recovered him of his swoon.

But when the King came to himself, he saw his foe lie, still as in death, on the ground beside him; and he was grieved, and said: "Merlin, what have ye done to this brave knight? Nay, if ye have slain him, I shall grieve my life long; for a good knight he is, bold and a fair fighter, though something wanting in knightly courtesy." "He is in better case than ye are, Sir King, who so lightly imperil your person, and thereby your kingdom's welfare; and, as ye say, Pellinore is a stout knight, and hereafter shall he serve you well. Have no fear. He shall wake again in three hours and have suffered naught by the encounter. But for you, it were well that ye came where ye might be tended for your wounds." "Nay," replied the King, smiling, "I may not return to my court thus weaponless; first will I find means to purvey me of a sword." "That is easily done," answered Merlin; "follow me, and I will bring you where ye shall get you a sword, the wonder of the world."

So, though his wounds pained him sore, the King followed Merlin by many a forest path and glade, until they came upon a mere, bosomed deep in the forest; and as he looked thereon, the King beheld an arm, clothed in white samite, shoot above the surface of the lake, and in the hand was a fair sword that gleamed in the level rays of the setting sun. "This is a great marvel," said the King, "what may it mean?" And Merlin made answer: "Deep is this mere, so deep indeed that no man may fathom it; but in its depths, and built upon the roots of the mountains, is the palace of the Lady of the Lake. Powerful is she with a power that works ever for good, and she shall help thee in thine hour of need. For thee has she wrought yonder sword. Go now, and take it."

Then was Arthur aware of a little skiff, half hidden among the bulrushes that fringed the lake; and leaping into the boat, without aid of oar, he was wafted out into the middle of the lake, to the place where, out of the water, rose the arm and sword. And leaning from the skiff, he took the sword from the hand, which forthwith vanished, and immediately thereafter the skiff bore him back to land.

Arthur drew from its scabbard the mighty sword, wondering the while at the marvel of its workmanship, for the hilt shone with the light of many twinkling gems—diamond and topaz and emerald, and many another whose names none know. And as he looked on the blade, Arthur was aware of mystic writings on the one side and the other, and calling to Merlin, he bade him interpret them. "Sir," said Merlin, "on the one side is written 'Keep me,' and on the other 'Throw me away.'" "Then," said the King, "which does it behove me to do?" "Keep it," answered Merlin; "the time to cast it away is not yet come. This is the good brand Excalibur, or Cut Steel, and well shall it serve you. But what think ye of the scabbard?" "A fair cover for so good a sword," answered Arthur. "Nay, it is more than that," said Merlin, "for, so long as ye keep it, though ye be wounded never so sore, yet ye shall not bleed to death." And when he heard that, the King marvelled the more.

Then they journeyed back to Caerleon, where the knights made great joy of the return of their lord. And presently, thither came Sir Pellinore, craving pardon of the King, who made but jest of his own misadventure. And afterwards Sir Pellinore became of the Table Round, a knight vowed, not only to deeds of hardihood, but also to gentleness and courtesy; and faithfully he served the King, fighting ever to maintain justice and put down wrong, and to defend the weak from the oppressor.

CHAPTER IV
OF THE TREACHERY OF
QUEEN MORGAN LE FAY

There was a certain Queen whose name was Morgan le Fay, and she was a powerful sorceress. Little do men know of her save that, in her youth, she was eager for knowledge and, having learnt all human lore, turned her to magic, becoming so skilled therein that she was feared of all. There was a time when great was her enmity towards King Arthur, so that she plotted his ruin not once only nor twice; and that is a strange thing, for it is said that she herself was the kinswoman of the King. And truly, in the end, she repented her of her malice, for she was, of those that came to bear Arthur to the Delightful Islands from the field of his last bitter conflict; but that was long after.

Now when this enchantress learned how the Lady of the Lake had given the King a sword and scabbard of strange might, she was filled with ill-will; and all her thought was only how she might wrest the weapon from him and have it for her own, to bestow as she would. Even while she pondered thereon, the King himself sent her the scabbard to keep for him; for Merlin never ceased to warn the King to have in safe keeping the scabbard that had power to keep him from mortal hurt; and it seemed to Arthur that none might better guard it for him, till the hour of need, than Morgan le Fay, the wise Queen that was of his own kindred. Yet was not the Queen shamed of her treacherous intent by the trust that Arthur had in her; but all her mind was set on how she might win to the possession of the sword itself as well as of the scabbard. At the last—so had her desire for the sword wrought upon her—she resolved to compass the destruction of the King that, if she gained the sword, never might she have need to fear his justice for the wrong she had done.

And her chance came soon. For, on a day, King Arthur resolved to chase the hart in the forests near Camelot, wherefore he left behind him his sword Excalibur, and took but a hunting spear with him. All day long, he chased a white hart and, when evening fell, he had far outstripped his attendants, save only two, Sir Accolon of Gaul and Sir Uriens, King of Gore, the husband of Queen Morgan le Fay herself. So when the King saw that darkness had come upon them in the forest, he turned to his companions, saying: "Sirs, we be far from Camelot and must lodge as we may this night. Let us go forward until we shall find where we may shelter us a little." So they rode forward, and presently Arthur espied a little lake glinting in the beams of the rising moon, and, as they drew nearer, they descried, full in the moonlight, a little ship, all hung with silks even to the water's edge. Then said the King to his knights: "Yonder is promise of shelter or, it may be, of adventure. Let us tether our horses in the thicket and enter into this little ship." And when they had so done, presently they found themselves in a fair cabin all hung with silks and tapestries, and, in its midst, a table spread with the choicest fare. And being weary and hungered with the chase, they ate of the feast prepared and, lying down to rest, were soon sunk in deep slumber.

While they slept, the little ship floated away from the land, and it came to pass that a great wonder befell; for when they woke in the morning, King Uriens found himself at home in his own land, and Sir Accolon was in his own chamber at Camelot; but the King lay a prisoner, bound and fettered and weaponless, in a noisome dungeon that echoed to the groans of hapless captives.

When he was come to himself, King Arthur looked about him and saw that his companions were knights in the same hard case as himself; and he inquired of them how they came to be in that plight. "Sir," said one of them, "we are in duresse in the castle of a certain recreant knight, Sir Damas by name, a coward false to chivalry. None love him, and so no champion can he find to maintain his cause in a certain quarrel that he has in hand. For this reason, he lies in wait with a great company of soldiers for any knights that may pass this way, and taking them prisoners, holds them in captivity unless they will undertake to fight to the death in his cause. And this I would not, nor any of my companions here; but unless we be speedily rescued, we are all like to die of hunger in this loathsome dungeon." "What is his quarrel?" asked the King. "That we none of us know," answered the knight.

While they yet talked, there entered the prison a damsel. She went up to the King at once, and said: "Knight, will ye undertake to fight in the cause of the lord of this castle?" "That I may not say," replied the King, "unless first I may hear what is his quarrel." "That ye shall not know," replied the damsel, "but this I tell you: if ye refuse, ye shall never leave this dungeon alive, but shall perish here miserably." "This is a hard case," said the King, "that I must either die or fight for one I know not, and in a cause that I may not hear. Yet on one condition will I undertake your lord's quarrel, and that is that he shall give me all the prisoners bound here in this dungeon." "It shall be as ye say," answered the damsel, "and ye shall also be furnished with horse and armour and sword than which ye never saw better." Therewith the damsel bade him follow her, and brought him to a great hall where presently there came to him squires to arm him for the combat; and when their service was rendered, the damsel said to him: "Sir Knight, even now there has come one who greets you in the name of Queen Morgan le Fay, and bids me tell you that the Queen, knowing your need, has sent you your good sword." Then the King rejoiced greatly, for it seemed to him that the sword that the damsel gave him was none other than the good sword Excalibur.

When all was prepared, the damsel led King Arthur into a fair field, and there he beheld awaiting him a knight, all sheathed in armour, his vizor down, and bearing a shield on which was no blazonry. So the two knights saluted each other, and, wheeling their horses, rode away from each other some little space.

Then turning again, they laid lance in rest, and rushing upon each other, encountered with the noise of thunder, and so great was the shock that each knight was borne from the saddle. Swiftly they gained their feet, and, drawing their swords, dealt each other great blows; and thus they contended fiercely for some while. But as he fought, a great wonder came upon Arthur, for it seemed to him that his sword, that never before had failed him, bit not upon the armour of the other, while every stroke of his enemy drew blood, till the ground on which he fought was slippery beneath his feet; and at the last almost his heart failed within him, knowing that he was betrayed, and that the brand with which he fought was not Excalibur. Yet would he not show aught of what he suffered, but struggled on, faint as he was and spent; so that they that watched the fight and saw how he was sore wounded, marvelled at his great courage and endurance. But presently, the stranger knight dealt the King a blow which fell upon Arthur's sword, and so fierce was the stroke that the blade broke off at the pommel. "Knight," said the other, "thou must yield thee recreant to my mercy." "That may I not do with mine honour," answered the King, "for I am sworn to fight in this quarrel to the death." "But weaponless thou must needs be slain." "Slay me an ye will, but think not to win glory by slaying a weaponless man."

Then was the other wroth to find himself still withstood and, in his anger, he dealt Arthur a great blow; but this the King shunned, and rushing upon his foe, smote him so fiercely on the head with the pommel of his broken sword that the knight swayed and let slip his own weapon. With a bound, Arthur was upon the sword, and no sooner had he it within his grasp than he knew it, of a truth, to be his own sword Excalibur. Then he scanned more closely his enemy, and saw the scabbard that he wore was none other than the magic scabbard of Excalibur; and forthwith, leaping upon the knight, he tore it from him and flung it far afield.

"Knight," cried King Arthur, "ye have made me suffer sore, but now is the case changed and ye stand within my power, helpless and unarmed. And much I misdoubt me but that treacherously ye have dealt with me. Nevertheless, yield you recreant and I will spare your life." "That I may not do, for it is against my vow; so slay me if ye will. Of a truth, ye are the best knight that ever I encountered."

Then it seemed to the King that the knight's voice was not unknown to him, and he said: "Tell me your name and what country ye are of, for something bids me think that ye are not all unknown to me." "I am Accolon of Gaul, knight of King Arthur's Round Table." "Ah! Accolon, Accolon," cried the King, "is it even thou that hast fought against me? Almost hast thou undone me. What treason tempted thee to come against me, and with mine own weapon too?" When Sir Accolon knew that it was against King Arthur that he had fought, he gave a loud cry and swooned away utterly. Then Arthur called to two stout yeomen amongst those that had looked on at the fight, and bade them bear Sir Accolon to a little hermitage hard by, and thither he himself followed with pain, being weak from loss of blood; but into the castle he would not enter, for he trusted not those that held it.

The hermit dressed their wounds, and presently, when Sir Accolon had come to himself again, the King spoke gently to him, bidding him say how he had come to bear arms against him. "Sir and my lord," answered Sir Accolon, "it comes of naught but the treachery of your kinswoman, Queen Morgan le Fay. For on the morrow after we had entered upon the little ship, I awoke in my chamber at Camelot, and greatly I marvelled how I had come there. And as I yet wondered, there came to me a messenger from Queen Morgan le Fay, desiring me to go to her without delay. And when I entered her presence, she was as one sore troubled, and she said to me: 'Sir Accolon, of my secret power, I know that now is our King, Arthur, in great danger; for he lies imprisoned in a great and horrible dungeon whence he may not be delivered unless one be found to do battle for him with the lord of the castle. Wherefore have I sent for you that ye may take the battle upon you for our lord the King. And for greater surety, I give you here Excalibur, Arthur's own sword, for, of a truth, we should use all means for the rescuing of our lord.' And I, believing this evil woman, came hither and challenged the lord of this castle to mortal combat; and, indeed, I deemed it was with Sir Damas that I fought even now. Yet all was treachery, and I misdoubt me that Sir Damas and his people are in league with Queen Morgan le Fay to compass your destruction. But, my lord Arthur, pardon me, I beseech you, the injuries that, all unwitting, I have done you."

King Arthur was filled with wrath against the Queen, more for the wrong done to Sir Accolon than for the treason to himself. In all ways that he might, he sought to comfort and relieve Sir Accolon, but in vain, for daily the knight grew weaker, and, after many days, he died. Then the King, being recovered of his wounds, returned to Camelot, and calling together a band of knights, led them against the castle of Sir Damas. But Damas had no heart to attempt to hold out, and surrendered himself and all that he had to the King's mercy. And first King Arthur set free those that Sir Damas had kept in miserable bondage, and sent them away with rich gifts. When he had righted the wrongs of others, then he summoned Sir Damas before him, and said: "I command thee that thou tell me why thou didst seek my destruction." And cringing low at the King's footstool, Damas answered: "I beseech you, deal mercifully with me, for all that I have done, I have done at the bidding of Queen Morgan le Fay." "A coward's plea," said the King; "how camest thou first to have traffic with her?" "Sir," replied Damas, "much have I suffered, first by the greed of my younger brother and now by the deceit of this evil woman, as ye shall hear. When my father died, I claimed the inheritance as of right, seeing that I was his elder son; but my young brother, Sir Ontzlake, withstood me, and demanded some part of my father's lands. Long since, he sent me a challenge to decide our quarrel in single combat, but it liked me ill, seeing that I am of no great strength. Much, therefore, did I desire to find a champion but, by ill fortune, none could I find until Queen Morgan le Fay sent word that, of her good will to me, she had sent me one that would defend my cause; and that same evening, the little ship brought you, my lord, to my castle. And when I saw you, I rejoiced, thinking to have found a champion that would silence my brother for ever; nor knew I you for the King's self. Wherefore, I entreat you, spare me, and avenge me on my brother." Therewith, Sir Damas fawned upon the King, but Arthur sternly bade him rise and send messengers to bring Sir Ontzlake before him.

Presently, there stood before the King a youth, fair and of good stature, who saluted his lord and then remained silent before him. "Sir Ontzlake," said the King, "I have sent for you to know of your dealings with Sir Accolon and of your quarrel with your brother." "My lord Arthur," answered the youth, "that I was the cause of hurt to yourself, I pray you to pardon me, for all unwitting was I of evil. For ye shall know that I had challenged my brother to single combat; but when word came to me that he was provided of a champion, I might not so much as brook my armour for a sore wound that I had got of an arrow shot at me as I rode through the forest near his castle. And as I grieved for my hard case, there came a messenger from Queen Morgan le Fay bidding me be of good courage, for she had sent unto me one, Sir Accolon, who would undertake my quarrel. This only she commanded me, that I should ask no question of Sir Accolon. So Sir Accolon abode with me that night and, as I supposed, fought in my cause the next day. Sure am I that there is some mystery, yet may I not misdoubt my lady Queen Morgan le Fay without cause; wherefore, if blame there be, let me bear the punishment."

Then was the King well pleased with the young man for his courage and loyalty to others. "Fair youth," said he, "ye shall go with me to Camelot, and if ye prove you brave and just in all your doings, ye shall be of my Round Table." But to Sir Damas he said sternly: "Ye are a mean-spirited varlet, unworthy of the degree of knighthood. Here I ordain that ye shall yield unto your brother the moiety of the lands that ye had of your father and, in payment for it, yearly ye shall receive of Sir Ontzlake a palfrey; for that will befit you better to ride than the knightly war-horse. And look ye well to it, on pain of death, that ye lie no more in wait for errant knights, but amend your life and live peaceably with your brother."

Thereafter, the fear of the King kept Sir Damas from deeds of violence; yet, to the end, he remained cowardly and churlish, unworthy of the golden spurs of knighthood. But Sir Ontzlake proved him a valiant knight, fearing God and the King and naught else.

CHAPTER V
HOW THE SCABBARD OF EXCALIBUR WAS LOST

Now when Queen Morgan le Fay knew that her plot had miscarried and that her treachery was discovered, she feared to abide the return of the King to Camelot; and so she went to Queen Guenevere, and said: "Madam, of your courtesy, grant me leave, I pray you, to depart." "Nay," said the Queen, "that were pity, for I have news of my lord the King, that soon he will return to Camelot. Will ye not then await his return, that ye may see your kinsman before ye depart?" "Alas! madam," said Morgan le Fay, "that may not be, for I have ill news that requires that immediately I get to my own country." "Then shall ye depart when ye will," said the Queen.

So before the next day had dawned, Morgan le Fay arose and, taking her horse, departed unattended from Camelot. All that day and most of the night she rode fast, and ere noon the next day, she was come to a nunnery where, as she knew, King Arthur lay. Entering into the house, she made herself known to the nuns, who received her courteously and gave her of their best to eat and to drink. When she was refreshed, she asked if any other had sought shelter with them that day; and they told her that King Arthur lay in an inner chamber and slept, for he had rested little for three nights. "Ah! my dear lord!" exclaimed the false sorceress; "gladly would I speak with him, but I will not that ye awaken him, and long I may not tarry here; wherefore suffer me at least to look upon him as he sleeps, and then will I continue my journey." And the nuns, suspecting no treachery, showed Queen Morgan le Fay the room where King Arthur slept, and let her enter it alone.

So Morgan le Fay had her will and stood beside the sleeping King; but again it seemed as if she must fail of her purpose, and her heart was filled with rage and despair. For she saw that the King grasped in his hand the hilt of the naked brand, that none might take it without awakening him. While she mused, suddenly she espied the scabbard where it hung at the foot of the bed, and her heart rejoiced to know that something she might gain by her bold venture. She snatched up the empty sheath, and wrapping it in a fold of her garment, left the chamber. Brief were her farewells to the holy nuns, and in haste she got to horse and rode away.

Scarcely had she set forth, when the King awoke, and rising from his couch, saw at once that the scabbard of his sword was gone. Then summoned he the whole household to his presence and inquired who had entered his chamber. "Sir," said the Abbess, "there has none been here save only your kinswoman, the Queen Morgan le Fay. She, indeed, desired to look upon you since she might not abide your awakening." Then the King groaned aloud, saying, "It is my own kinswoman, the wife of my true knight, Sir Uriens, that would betray me." He bade Sir Ontzlake make ready to accompany him, and after courteous salutation to the Abbess and her nuns, together they rode forth by the path that Morgan le Fay had taken.

Fast they rode in pursuit, and presently they came to a cross where was a poor cowherd keeping watch over his few beasts, and of him they asked whether any had passed that way. "Sirs," said the peasant, "even now there rode past the cross a lady most lovely to look upon, and with her forty knights." Greatly the King marvelled how Queen Morgan le Fay had come by such a cavalcade, but nothing he doubted that it was she the cowherd had seen. So thanking the poor man, the King, with Sir Ontzlake, rode on by the path that had been shown them, and presently, emerging from the forest, they were aware of a glittering company of horsemen winding through a wide plain that lay stretched before them. On the instant, they put spurs to their horses and galloped as fast as they might in pursuit.

But, as it chanced, Queen Morgan le Fay looked back even as Arthur and Sir Ontzlake came forth from the forest, and seeing them, she knew at once that her theft had been discovered, and that she was pursued. Straightway she bade her knights ride on till they should come to a narrow valley where lay many great stones; but as soon as they had left her, she herself rode, with all speed, to a mere hard by. Sullen and still it lay, without even a ripple on its surface. No animal ever drank of its waters nor bird sang by it, and it was so deep that none might ever plumb it. And when the Queen had come to the brink, she dismounted. From the folds of her dress she drew the scabbard, and waving it above her head, she cried, "Whatsoever becometh of me, King Arthur shall not have this scabbard." Then, whirling it with all her might, she flung it far into the mere. The jewels glinted as the scabbard flashed through the air, then it clove the oily waters of the lake and sank, never again to be seen.

When it had vanished, Morgan le Fay mounted her horse again, and rode fast after her knights, for the King and Ontzlake were in hot pursuit, and sore she feared lest they should come up with her before she might reach the shelter of the Valley of Stones. But she had rejoined her company of knights before the King had reached the narrow mouth of the valley. Quickly she bade her men scatter among the boulders, and then, by her magic art, she turned them all, men and horses and herself too, into stones, that none might tell the one from the other.

When King Arthur and Sir Ontzlake reached the valley, they looked about for some sign of the presence of the Queen or her knights, but naught might they see though they rode through the valley and beyond, and returning, searched with all diligence among the rocks and boulders. Never again was Queen Morgan le Fay seen at Camelot, nor did she attempt aught afterwards against the welfare of the King. When she had restored her knights to their proper form, she hastened with them back to her own land, and there she abode for the rest of her days until she came with the other queens to carry Arthur from the field of the Battle in the West.

Nor would the King seek to take vengeance on a woman, though sorely she had wronged him. His life long, he guarded well the sword Excalibur, but the sheath no man ever saw again.

CHAPTER VI
MERLIN

Of Merlin and how he served King Arthur, something has been already shown. Loyal he was ever to Uther Pendragon and to his son, King Arthur, and for the latter especially he wrought great marvels. He brought the King to his rights; he made him his ships; and some say that Camelot, with its splendid halls, where Arthur would gather his knights around him at the great festivals of the year, at Christmas, at Easter, and at Pentecost, was raised by his magic, without human toil. Bleise, the aged magician who dwelt in Northumberland and recorded the great deeds of Arthur and his knights, had been Merlin's master in magic; but it came to pass in time that Merlin far excelled him in skill, so that his enemies declared no mortal was his father, and called him devil's son.

Then, on a certain time, Merlin said to Arthur: "The time draws near when ye shall miss me, for I shall go down alive into the earth; and it shall be that gladly would ye give your lands to have me again." Then Arthur was grieved, and said: "Since ye know your danger, use your craft to avoid it." But Merlin answered: "That may not be."

Now there had come to Arthur's court, a damsel of the Lady of the Lake — her whose skill in magic, some say, was greater than Merlin's own; and the damsel's name was Vivien. She set herself to learn the secrets of Merlin's art, and was ever with him, tending upon the old man and, with gentleness and tender service, winning her way to his heart; but all was a pretence, for she was weary of him and sought only his ruin, thinking it should be fame for her, by any means whatsoever, to enslave the greatest wizard of his age. And so she persuaded him to pass with her overseas into

King Ban's land of Benwick, and there, one day, he showed her a wondrous rock, formed by magic art. Then she begged him to enter into it, the better to declare to her its wonders; but when once he was within, by a charm that she had learnt from Merlin's self, she caused the rock to shut down that never again might he come forth. Thus was Merlin's prophecy fulfilled, that he should go down into the earth alive. Much they marvelled in Arthur's court what had become of the great magician, till on a time, there rode past the stone a certain Knight of the Round Table and heard Merlin lamenting his sad fate. The knight would have striven to raise the mighty stone, but Merlin bade him not waste his labour, since none might release him save her who had imprisoned him there. Thus Merlin passed from the world through the treachery of a damsel, and thus Arthur was without aid in the days when his doom came upon him.

CHAPTER VII
BALIN AND BALAN

Among the princes that thought scorn of Arthur in the days when first he became king, none was more insolent than Ryons of North Wales. So, on a time when King Arthur held high festival at Camelot, Ryons sent a herald who, in the presence of the whole court, before brave knights and fair dames, thus addressed the King: "Sir Arthur, my master bids me say that he has overcome eleven kings with all their hosts, and, in token of their submission, they have given him their beards to fringe him a mantle. There remains yet space for the twelfth; wherefore, with all speed, send him your beard, else will he lay waste your land with fire and sword." "Viler message," said King Arthur, "was never sent from man to man. Get thee gone, lest we forget thine office protects thee." So spoke the King, for he had seen his knights clap hand to sword, and would not that a messenger should suffer hurt in his court.

Now among the knights present the while was one whom men called Balin le Savage, who had but late been freed from prison for slaying a knight of Arthur's court. None was more wroth than he at the villainy of Ryons, and immediately after the departure of the herald, he left the hall and armed him; for he was minded to try if, with good fortune, he might win to Arthur's grace by avenging him on the King of North Wales. While he was without, there entered the hall a Witch Lady who, on a certain occasion, had done the King a service, and for this she now desired of him a boon. So Arthur bade her name her request, and thus she said: "O King, I require of you the head of the knight Balin le Savage." "That may I not grant you with my honour," replied the King; "ask what it may become me to give." But the Witch Lady would have naught else, and departed from the hall, murmuring against the King. Then, as it chanced, Balin met her at the door, and immediately when he saw her, he rode upon her, sword in hand, and, with one blow, smote off her head. Thus he took vengeance for his mother's death, of which she had been the cause, and, well content, rode away. But when it was told King Arthur of the deed that Balin had done, he was full wroth, nor was his anger lessened though Merlin declared the wrong the Witch Lady had done to Balin. "Whatsoever cause he had against her, yet should he have done her no violence in my court," said the King, and bade Sir Lanceour of Ireland ride after Balin and bring him back again.

Thus it came to pass that, as Sir Balin rode on his way, he heard the hoof-beats of a horse fast galloping, and a voice cried loudly to him: "Stay, Knight; for thou shalt stay, whether thou wilt or not." "Fair Knight," answered Balin fiercely, "dost thou desire to fight with me?" "Yea, truly," answered Lanceour; "for that cause have I followed thee from Camelot." "Alas!" cried Balin, "then I know thy quarrel. And yet, I dealt but justly by that vile woman, and it grieves me to offend my lord King Arthur again." "Have done, and make ready to fight," said Lanceour insolently; for he was proud and arrogant, though a brave knight. So they rushed together, and, at the first encounter, Sir Lanceour's spear was shivered against the shield of the other, but Balin's spear pierced shield and hauberk and Lanceour fell dead to the earth.

Then Sir Balin, sore grieved that he had caused the death of a knight of Arthur's court, buried Lanceour as well as he might, and continued sorrowfully on his journey in search of King Ryons. Presently, as he rode through a great forest, he espied a knight whom, by his arms, he knew at once for his brother, Sir Balan. Great joy had they in their meeting, for Balan had believed Balin still to be in prison. So Balin told Balan all that had befallen him, and how he sought Ryons to avenge Arthur upon him for his insolent message, and hoped thereby to win his lord's favour again. "I will ride with thee, brother," said Balan, "and help thee all I may." So the two went on their way till, presently, they met with an old man—Merlin's self, though they knew him not, for he was disguised. "Ah, Knight," said Merlin to Balin, "swift to strike and swift to repent, beware, or thou shalt strike the most dolorous blow dealt by man; for thou shalt slay thine own brother." "If I believed thy words true," cried Balin hotly, "I would slay myself to make thee a liar." "I know the past and I know the future," said Merlin; "I know, too, the errand on which thou ridest, and I will help thee if thou wilt." "Ah!" said Balin, "that pleases me well." "Hide you both in this covert," said Merlin; "for presently there shall come riding down this path King Ryons with sixty of his knights." With these words he vanished. So Balin and Balan did as he had bidden them, and when King Ryons and his men entered the little path, they fell upon them with such fury that they slew more than forty knights, while the rest fled, and King Ryons himself yielded him to them. So Sir Balan rode with King Ryons to Camelot that he might deliver him to King Arthur; but Balin went not with them, for he would see more adventures before he sought King Arthur's presence again.

After many days' travel and many encounters, it befell that, one evening, Balin drew near to a castle; and when he would have sought admittance, there stood by him an old man, and said: "Balin, turn thee back, and it shall be better for thee," and so vanished. At that moment there was blown a blast on a horn, such as is sounded when the stag receives its death; and hearing it, Balin's heart misgave him, and he cried: "That blast is blown for me, and I am the prize. But not yet am I dead!"

At that instant the castle gate was raised and there appeared many knights and ladies welcoming Balin into the castle. So he entered, and presently they were all seated at supper. Then the lady of the castle said to Balin: "Sir Knight, to-morrow thou must have ado with a knight that keeps an island near-by; else mayest thou not pass that way." "That is an evil custom," answered Balin; "but if I must, I must." So that night he rested, but with the dawn he arose, and was arming himself for battle when there came to him a knight and said: "Sir, your shield is not good; I pray you, take mine which is larger and stouter." In an evil hour, Balin suffered himself to be persuaded, and taking the stranger's shield, left; behind his own on which his arms were blazoned. Then, entering a boat, he was conveyed to the island where the unknown knight held the ford.

No sooner was he landed, than there came riding to him a knight armed all in red armour, his horse, too, trapped all in red; and without word spoken, they charged upon each other, and each bore the other from the saddle. Thus for a while they lay, stunned by the fall. The Red Knight was the first to rise, for Balin, all wearied by his travels and many encounters, was sore shaken by the fall. Then they fought together right fiercely, hacking away great pieces of armour, and dealing each other dreadful wounds. But when they paused to take breath, Balin, looking up, saw the battlements of the castle filled with knights and ladies watching the struggle, and immediately, shamed that the conflict should have so long endured, he rushed again upon the Red Knight, aiming at him blows that might have felled a giant. So they fought together a long while; but at the last, the Red Knight drew back a little. Then cried Balin: "Who art thou? for till now, never have I met my match." Then said the Red Knight: "I am Balan, brother to the noble knight, Sir Balin"; and with the word, he fell to the ground as one dead. "Alas!" cried Balin, "that I should have lived to see this day!" Then, as well as he might, for his strength was almost spent, he crept on hands and knees to his brother's side and opened the vizor of his helmet, and when he saw his brother's face all ghastly, as it was, he cried: "O Balan, I have slain thee, as thou hast also slain me! Oh! woeful deed I never to be forgotten of men!" Then Balan, being somewhat recovered, told Balin how he had been compelled by those at the castle to keep the ford against all comers, and might never depart; and Balin told of the grievous chance by which he had taken another's shield.

So these two died, slain by each other's hands. In one tomb they were buried; and Merlin, passing that way, inscribed thereon the full story of their deaths.

BOOK II
SIR LAUNCELOT

CHAPTER VIII
SIR LAUNCELOT DU LAC

Now, as time passed, King Arthur gathered into his Order of the Round Table knights whose peers shall never be found in any age; and foremost amongst them all was Sir Launcelot du Lac. Such was his strength that none against whom he laid lance in rest could keep the saddle, and no shield was proof against his sword dint; but for his courtesy even more than for his courage and strength, Sir Launcelot was famed far and near. Gentle he was and ever the first to rejoice in the renown of another; and in the jousts, he would avoid encounter with the young and untried knight, letting him pass to gain glory if he might.

It would take a great book to record all the famous deeds of Sir Launcelot, and all his adventures. He was of Gaul, for his father, King Ban, ruled over Benwick; and some say that his first name was Galahad, and that he was named Launcelot du Lac by the Lady of the Lake who reared him when his mother died. Early he won renown by delivering his father's people from the grim King Claudas who, for more than twenty years, had laid waste the fair land of Benwick; then, when there was peace in his own land, he passed into Britain, to Arthur's court, where the King received him gladly, and made him Knight of the Round Table and took him for his trustiest friend. And so it was that, when Guenevere was to be brought to Canterbury, to be married to the King, Launcelot was chief of the knights sent to wait upon her, and of this came the sorrow of later days. For, from the moment he saw her, Sir Launcelot loved Guenevere, for her sake remaining wifeless all his days, and in all things being her faithful knight. But busybodies and mischief-makers spoke evil of Sir Launcelot and the Queen, and from their talk came the undoing of the King and the downfall of his great work. But that was after long years, and after many true knights had lived their lives, honouring the King and Queen, and doing great deeds whereby the fame of Arthur and his Order passed through all the world.

CHAPTER IX
THE ADVENTURE OF THE
CHAPEL PERILOUS

Now on a day, as he rode through the forest, Sir Launcelot met a damsel weeping bitterly, and seeing him, she cried, "Stay, Sir Knight! By your knighthood I require you to aid me in my distress." Immediately Sir Launcelot checked his horse and asked in what she needed his service. "Sir," said the maiden, "my brother lies at the point of death, for this day he fought with the stout knight, Sir Gilbert, and sorely they wounded each other; and a wise woman, a sorceress, has said that nothing may staunch my brother's wounds unless they be searched with the sword and bound up with a piece of the cloth from the body of the wounded knight who lies in the ruined chapel hard by. And well I know you, my lord Sir Launcelot, and that, if ye will not help me, none may." "Tell me your brother's name," said Sir Launcelot. "Sir Meliot de Logris," answered the damsel. "A Knight of our Round Table," said Sir Launcelot; "the more am I bound to your service. Only tell me, gentle damsel, where I may find this Chapel Perilous." So she directed him, and, riding through forest byeways, Sir Launcelot came presently upon a little ruined chapel, standing in the midst of a churchyard, where the tombs showed broken and neglected under the dark yews. In front of the porch, Sir Launcelot paused and looked, for thereon hung, upside down, dishonoured, the shield of many a good knight whom Sir Launcelot had known.

As he stood wondering, suddenly there pressed upon him from all sides thirty stout knights, all giants and fully armed, their drawn swords in their hands and their shields advanced. With threatening looks, they spoke to him saying: "Sir Launcelot, it were well ye turned back before evil befell you." But Sir Launcelot, though he feared to have to do with thirty such warriors, answered boldly: "I turn not back for high words. Make them good by your deeds." Then he rode upon them fiercely, whereupon instantly they scattered and disappeared, and, sword in hand, Sir Launcelot entered the little chapel. All was dark within, save that a little lamp hung from the roof, and by its dim light he could just espy how on a bier before the altar there lay, stark and cold, a knight sheathed in armour. And drawing nearer, Sir Launcelot saw that the dead man lay on a blood-stained mantle, his naked sword by his side, but that his left hand had been lopped off at the wrist by a mighty sword-cut. Then Sir Launcelot boldly seized the sword and with it cut off a piece of the bloody mantle. Immediately the earth shook and the walls of the chapel rocked, and in fear Sir Launcelot turned to go. But, as he would have left the chapel, there stood before him in the doorway a lady, fair to look upon and beautifully arrayed, who gazed earnestly upon him, and said: "Sir Knight, put away from you that sword lest it be your death." But Sir Launcelot answered her: "Lady, what I have said, I do; and what I have won, I keep." "It is well," said the lady. "Had ye cast away the sword your life days were done. And now I make but one request. Kiss me once." "That may I not do," said Sir Launcelot. Then said the lady: "Go your way, Launcelot; ye have won, and I have lost. Know that, had ye kissed me, your dead body had lain even now on the altar bier. For much have I desired to win you; and to entrap you, I ordained this chapel. Many a knight have I taken, and once Sir Gawain himself hardly escaped, but he fought with Sir Gilbert and lopped off his hand, and so got away. Fare ye well; it is plain to see that none but our lady, Queen Guenevere, may have your services." With that, she vanished from his sight. So Sir Launcelot mounted his horse and rode away from that evil place till he met Sir Meliot's sister, who led him to her brother where he lay, pale as the earth, and bleeding fast. And when he saw Sir Launcelot, he would have risen to greet him; but his strength failed him, and he fell back on his couch. Sir Launcelot searched his wounds with the sword, and bound them up with the blood-stained cloth, and immediately Sir Meliot was sound and well, and greatly he rejoiced. Then Sir Meliot and his sister begged Sir Launcelot to stay and rest, but he departed on his adventures, bidding them farewell until he should meet them again at Arthur's court.

As for the sorceress of the Chapel Perilous, it is said she died of grief that all her charms had failed to win for her the good knight Sir Launcelot.

CHAPTER X
SIR LAUNCELOT AND THE FALCON

Sir Launcelot rode on his way, by marsh and valley and hill, till he chanced upon a fair castle, and saw fly from it, over his head, a beautiful falcon, with the lines still hanging from her feet. And as he looked, the falcon flew into a tree where she was held fast by the lines becoming entangled about the boughs. Immediately, from the castle there came running a fair lady, who cried: "O Launcelot, Launcelot! As ye are the noblest of all knights, I pray you help me to recover my falcon. For if my husband discover its loss, he will slay me in his anger." "Who is your husband, fair lady?" asked Sir Launcelot. "Sir Phelot, a knight of Northgalis, and he is of a hasty temper; wherefore, I beseech you, help me." "Well, lady," said Sir Launcelot, "I will serve you if I may; but the tree is hard to climb, for the boughs are few, and, in truth, I am no climber. But I will do my best." So the lady helped Sir Launcelot to unarm, and he led his horse to the foot of the tree, and springing from its back, he caught at the nearest bough, and drew himself up into the branches. Then he climbed till he reached the falcon and, tying her lines to a rotten bough, broke it off, and threw down bird and bough to the lady below. Forthwith, Sir Phelot came from amongst the trees and said: "Ah! Sir Launcelot! Now at length I have you as I would; for I have long sought your life." And Sir Launcelot made answer: "Surely ye would not slay me, an unarmed man; for that were dishonour to you. Keep my armour if ye will; but hang my sword on a bough where I may reach it, and then do with me as ye can." But Sir Phelot laughed mockingly and said: "Not so, Sir Launcelot. I know you too well to throw away my advantage; wherefore, shift as ye may." "Alas!" said Sir Launcelot, "that ever knight should be so unknightly. And you, madam, how could ye so betray me?" "She did but as I commanded her," said Sir Phelot.

Then Launcelot looked about him to see how he might help himself in these straits, and espying above his head a great bare branch, he tote it down. Then, ever watching his advantage, he sprang to the ground on the far side of his horse, so that the horse was between him and Sir Phelot. Sir Phelot rushed upon him with his sword, but Sir Launcelot parried it with the bough, with which he dealt his enemy such a blow on the head that Sir Phelot sank to the ground in a swoon. Then Sir Launcelot seized his sword where it lay beside his armour, and stooping over the fallen knight, unloosed his helm. When the lady saw him do that, she shrieked and cried: "Spare his life! spare his life, noble knight, I beseech you!" But Sir Launcelot answered sternly: "A felon's death for him who does felon's deeds. He has lived too long already," and with one blow, he smote off his head. Then he armed himself, and mounting upon his steed, rode away, leaving the lady to weep beside her lord.

BOOK III
SIR TRISTRAM

CHAPTER XI
OF THE BIRTH OF SIR TRISTRAM

In the days of Arthur, there ruled over the kingdom of Liones the good knight Sir Meliodas; and his Queen was the fair Elizabeth, sister of King Mark of Cornwall.

Now there was a lady, an enchantress, who had no good-will towards King Meliodas and his Queen; so one day, when the King was hunting, she brought it to pass by her charms that Meliodas chased a hart till he found himself, far from all his men, alone by an old castle, and there he was taken prisoner by the lady's knights.

When King Meliodas did not return home, the Queen was nigh crazed with grief. Attended only by one of the ladies of her court, she ran out into the forest to seek her lord. Long and far she wandered, until she could go no further, but sank down at the foot of a great tree, and there, in the midst of the forest, was her little son born. When the Queen knew that she must die, she kissed the babe and said: "Ah! little son, sad has been thy birth, wherefore thy name shall be Tristram; but thou shalt grow to be a brave knight and a strong." Then she charged her gentlewoman to take care of the child and to commend her to King Meliodas; and after that she died. All too late came many of the barons seeking their Queen, and sorrowfully they bore her back to the castle where presently the King arrived, released by the skill of Merlin from the evil spells of the enchantress. Great indeed was his grief for the death of his Queen. He caused her to be buried with all the pomp and reverence due to so good and fair a lady, and long and bitterly he mourned her loss and all the people with him.

But at the end of seven years, King Meliodas took another wife. Then, when the Queen had sons of her own, it angered her to think that in the days to come, her stepson Tristram, and none other, should rule the fair land of Liones. The more she thought of it, the more she hated him till, at the last, she was resolved to do away with him. So she filled a silver goblet with a pleasant drink in which she had mixed poison, and she set it in the room where Tristram played with the young princes, his half-brothers. Now the day was hot, and presently, being heated with his play, the young prince, the Queen's eldest son, drank of the poisoned goblet; and immediately he died. Much the Queen grieved, but more than ever she hated her stepson Tristram, as if, through him, her son had died. Presently, again she mixed poison and set it in a goblet; and that time, King Meliodas, returning thirsty from the chase, took the cup and would have drunk of it, only the Queen cried to him to forbear. Then the King recalled to mind how his young son had drunk of a seeming pleasant drink and died on the instant; and seizing the Queen by the hand, he cried: "False traitress! tell me at once what is in that cup, or I will slay thee!" Then the Queen cried him mercy and told him all her sin. But in his wrath the King would have no mercy, but sentenced her to be burnt at the stake, which, in those days, was the doom of traitors. The day having come when the Queen should suffer for her fault, she was led out and bound to a stake in the presence of all the court, and the faggots were heaped about her. Then the young prince Tristram kneeled before the King and asked of him a favour: and the King, loving him much, granted him his request. "Then," said Tristram, "I require you to release the Queen, my stepmother, and to take her again to your favour." Greatly the King marvelled, and said: "Ye should of right hate her, seeing that she sought your life." But Tristram answered: "I forgive her freely." "I give you then her life," said the King; "do ye release her from the stake." So Tristram unloosed the chains which bound the Queen and led her back to the castle, and from that day the Queen loved him well; but as for King Meliodas, though he forgave her and suffered her to remain at court, yet never again would he have aught to do with her.

CHAPTER XII
HOW TRISTRAM FOUGHT WITH SIR MARHAUS OF IRELAND

Now King Meliodas, though he had pardoned the Queen, would keep his son Tristram no longer at the court, but sent him into France. There Tristram learnt all knightly exercises, so that there was none could equal him as harper or hunter; and after seven years, being by then a youth of nineteen, he returned to his own land of Liones.

It chanced, in those days, that King Anguish of Ireland sent to Cornwall, demanding the tribute paid him in former times by that land. Then Mark, the Cornish King, called together his barons and knights to take counsel; and by their advice, he made answer that he would pay no tribute, and bade King Anguish send a stout knight to fight for his right if he still dared claim aught of the land of Cornwall.

Forthwith there came from Ireland Sir Marhaus, brother of the Queen of Ireland. Now Sir Marhaus was Knight of the Round Table and in his time there were few of greater renown. He anchored his ships under the Castle of Tintagil, and sent messengers daily to King Mark, bidding him pay the tribute or find one to fight in his cause.

Then was King Mark sore perplexed, for not one of his knights dared encounter Sir Marhaus. Criers were sent through all the land, proclaiming that, to any knight that would take the combat upon him, King Mark would give such gifts as should enrich him for life. In time, word of all that had happened came to Liones, and immediately Tristram sought his father, desiring his permission to go to the court of his uncle, King Mark, to take the battle upon him. Thus it came to pass that, with his father's good leave, Tristram presented himself before King Mark, asking to be made knight that he might do battle for the liberties of Cornwall. Then when Mark knew that it was his sister's son, he rejoiced greatly, and having made Tristram knight, he sent word to Sir Marhaus that there was found to meet him a champion of better birth than Sir Marhaus' self.

So it was arranged that the combat should take place on a little island hard by, where Sir Marhaus had anchored his ships. Sir Tristram, with his horse and arms, was placed on board a ship, and when the island was gained, he leaped on shore, bidding his squire put off again and only return when he was slain or victorious.

Now, when Sir Marhaus saw that Tristram was but a youth, he cried aloud to him: "Be advised, young Sir, and go back to your ship. What can ye hope to do against me, a proven knight of Arthur's Table?" Then Tristram made answer: "Sir and most famous champion, I have been made knight to do battle with you, and I promise myself to win honour thereby, I who have never before encountered a proven knight." "If ye can endure three strokes of my sword, it shall be honour enough," said Sir Marhaus. Then they rushed upon each other, and at the first encounter each unhorsed the other, and Sir Marhaus' spear pierced Sir Tristram's side and made a grievous wound. Drawing their swords, they lashed at each other, and the blows fell thick as hail till the whole island re-echoed with the din of onslaught. So they fought half a day, and ever it seemed that Sir Tristram grew fresher and nimbler while Sir Marhaus became sore wearied. And at the last, Sir Tristram aimed a great blow at the head of his enemy, and the sword crashed through the helmet and bit into the skull so that a great piece was broken away from the edge of Tristram's sword. Then Sir Marhaus flung away sword and shield, and when he might regain his feet, fled shrieking to his ships. "Do ye flee?" cried Tristram. "I am but newly made knight; but rather than flee, I would be hewn piecemeal."

Then came Gouvernail, Sir Tristram's squire, and bore his master back to land, where Mark and all the Cornish lords came to meet him and convey him to the castle of Tintagil. Far and wide they sent for surgeons to dress Sir Tristram's wound, but none might help him, and ever he grew weaker. At the last, a wise woman told King Mark that in that land alone whence came the poisoned spear could Sir Tristram find cure. Then the King gave orders and a ship was made ready with great stores of rich furnishings, to convey Sir Tristram to Ireland, there to heal him of his wound.

CHAPTER XIII
THE FAIR ISOLT

Thus Tristram sailed to Ireland, and when he drew nigh the coast, he called for his harp, and sitting up on his couch on the deck, played the merriest tune that was ever heard in that land. And the warders on the castle wall, hearing him, sent and told King Anguish how a ship drew near with one who harped as none other might. Then King Anguish sent knights to convey the stranger into the castle. So when he was brought into the King's presence, Tristram declared that he was Sir Tramtrist of Liones, lately made knight, and wounded in his first battle; for which cause he was come to Ireland, to seek healing. Forthwith the King made him welcome, and placed him in the charge of his daughter, Isolt. Now Isolt was famed for her skill in surgery, and, moreover, she was the fairest lady of that time, save only Queen Guenevere. So she searched and bandaged Sir Tristram's wound, and presently it was healed. But still Sir Tristram abode at King Anguish's court, teaching the Fair Isolt to harp, and taking great pleasure in her company. And ever the princess doubted whether Sir Tristram were not a renowned knight and ever she liked him better.

So the time passed merrily with feastings and in the jousts, and in the lists Sir Tristram won great honour when he was recovered of his wound.

At last it befell upon a day that Sir Tristram had gone to the bath and left his sword lying on the couch. And the Queen, entering, espied it, and taking it up, drew the sword from the sheath and fell to admiring the mighty blade. Presently she saw that the edge was notched, and while she pondered how great a blow must have broken the good steel, suddenly she bethought her of the piece which had been found in the head of her brother, Sir Marhaus. Hastening to her chamber, she sought in a casket for the fragment, and returning, placed it by the sword edge, where it fitted as well as on the day it was first broken. Then she cried to her daughter: "This, then, is the traitor knight who slew my brother, Sir Marhaus"; and snatching up the sword, she rushed upon Sir Tristram where he sat in his bath, and would have killed him, but that his squire restrained her. Having failed of her purpose, she sought her husband, King Anguish, and told him all her story: how the knight they had harboured was he who had slain Sir Marhaus. Then the King, sore perplexed, went to Sir Tristram's chamber, where he found him fully armed, ready to get to horse. And Tristram told him all the truth, how in fair fight he had slain Sir Marhaus. "Ye did as a knight should," said King Anguish; "and much it grieves me that I may not keep you at my court; but I cannot so displease my Queen or barons." "Sir," said Tristram, "I thank you for your courtesy, and will requite it as occasion may offer. Moreover, here I pledge my word, as I am good knight and true, to be your daughter's servant, and in all places and at all times to uphold her quarrel. Wherefore I pray you that I may take my leave of the princess."

Then, with the King's permission, Sir Tristram went to the Fair Isolt and told her all his story; "And here," said he, "I make my vow ever to be your true knight, and at all times and in all places to uphold your quarrel." "And on my part" answered the Fair Isolt, "I make promise that never these seven years will I marry any man, save with your leave and as ye shall desire." Therewith they exchanged rings, the Fair Isolt grieving sore the while. Then Sir Tristram strode into the court and cried aloud, before all the barons: "Ye knights of Ireland, the time is come when I must depart. Therefore, if any man have aught against me, let him stand forth now, and I will satisfy him as I may." Now there were many present of the kin of Sir Marhaus, but none dared have ado with Sir Tristram; so, slowly he rode away, and with his squire took ship again for Cornwall.

CHAPTER XIV
HOW KING MARK SENT SIR TRISTRAM TO FETCH HIM A WIFE

When Sir Tristram had come back to Cornwall, he abode some time at the court of King Mark. Now in those days the Cornish knights were little esteemed, and none less than Mark himself, who was a coward, and never adventured himself in fair and open combat, seeking rather to attack by stealth and have his enemy at an advantage. But the fame of Sir Tristram increased daily, and all men spoke well of him. So it came to pass that King Mark, knowing himself despised, grew fearful and jealous of the love that all men bore his nephew; for he seemed in their praise of him to hear his own reproach. He sought, therefore, how he might rid himself of Tristram even while he spoke him fair and made as if he loved him much, and at the last he bethought him how he might gain his end and no man be the wiser. So one day, he said to Tristram: "Fair nephew, I am resolved to marry, and fain would I have your aid." "In all things, I am yours to command," answered Sir Tristram. "I pray you, then," said King Mark, "bring me to wife the Fair Isolt of Ireland. For since I have heard your praises of her beauty, I may not rest unless I have her for my Queen." And this he said thinking that, if ever Sir Tristram set foot in Ireland, he would be slain.

But Tristram, nothing mistrusting, got together a company of gallant knights, all fairly arrayed as became men sent by their King on such an errand; and with them he embarked on a goodly ship. Now it chanced that when he had reached the open sea, a great storm arose and drove him back on to the coast of England, and landing with great difficulty he set up his pavilion hard by the city of Camelot.

Presently, word was brought him by his squire that King Anguish with his company lay hard by, and that the King was in sore straits; for he was charged with the murder of a knight of Arthur's court, and must meet in combat Sir Blamor, one of the stoutest knights of the Round Table. Then Sir Tristram rejoiced, for he saw in this opportunity of serving King Anguish the means of earning his good will. So he betook himself to the King's tent, and proffered to take upon him the encounter, for the kindness shown him by King Anguish in former days. And the King gratefully accepting of his championship, the next day Sir Tristram encountered with Sir Blamor, overthrew him, and so acquitted the Irish King of the charge brought against him. Then in his joy, King Anguish begged Sir Tristram to voyage with him to his own land, bidding Tristram ask what boon he would and he should have it. So rejoicing in his great fortune, Sir Tristram sailed once again for the Irish land.

CHAPTER XV
HOW SIR TRISTRAM AND THE FAIR ISOLT DRANK OF THE MAGIC POTION

Then King Anguish made haste to return to Ireland, taking Sir Tristram with him. And when he was come there and had told all his adventures, there was great rejoicing over Sir Tristram, but of none more than of the Fair Isolt. So when Sir Tristram had stayed there some while, King Anguish reminded him of the boon he should ask and of his own willingness to grant it. "Sir King," replied Sir Tristram, "now will I ask it. Grant me your daughter, the Fair Isolt, that I may take her to Cornwall, there to become the wife of my uncle, King Mark." Then King Anguish grieved when he heard Sir Tristram's request, and said: "Far more gladly would I give her to you to wife." "That may not be," replied Sir Tristram; "my honour forbids." "Take her then," said King Anguish, "she is yours to wed or to give to your uncle, King Mark, as seems good to you."

So a ship was made ready and there entered it the Fair Isolt and Sir Tristram, and Gouvernail, his squire, and Dame Bragwaine, who was maid to the princess. But before they sailed, the Queen gave in charge to Gouvernail and Dame Bragwaine a phial of wine which King Mark and Isolt should drink together on their wedding-day; "For," said the Queen, "such is the magic virtue of this wine, that, having drunk of it, they may never cease from loving one another."

Now it chanced, one day, that Sir Tristram sat and harped to the Fair Isolt; and the weather being hot, he became thirsty. Then looking round the cabin he beheld a golden flask, curiously shaped and wrought; and laughing, he said to the Fair Isolt: "See, madam, how my man and your maid care for themselves; for here is the best wine that ever I tasted. I pray you, now, drink to me." So with mirth and laughter, they pledged each other, and thought that never before had they tasted aught so good. But when they had made an end of drinking, there came upon them the might of the magic charm; and never from that day, for good or for ill, might they cease from their love. And so much woe was wrought; for, mindful of his pledge to his uncle, Sir Tristram brought Isolt in all honour into the land of Cornwall where she was wedded with pomp and ceremony to King Mark, the craven King, who hated his nephew even more than before, because he had returned in safety and made good his promise as became an honourable knight. And from that day he never ceased seeking the death of Sir Tristram.

CHAPTER XVI
OF THE END OF SIR TRISTRAM

Then again Sir Tristram abode at King Mark's court, ever rendering the Fair Isolt loyal and knightly service; for King Mark would imperil his life for none, no matter what the need.

Now among the Cornish knights, there was much jealousy of Sir Tristram de Liones, and chief of his enemies was his own cousin, Sir Andred. With lying words, Sir Andred sought to stir up King Mark against his nephew, speaking evil of the Queen and of Sir Tristram. Now Mark was afraid openly to accuse Sir Tristram, so he set Sir Andred to spy upon him. At last, it befell one day that Sir Andred saw Sir Tristram coming, alone and unarmed, from the Queen's presence, and with twelve other knights, he fell upon him and bound him. Then these felon knights bore Sir Tristram to a little chapel standing upon a great rock which jutted out into the sea. There they would have slain him, unarmed and bound. But Sir Tristram, perceiving their intent, put forth suddenly all his strength, burst his bonds, and wresting a sword from Sir Andred, cut him down; and so he did with six other knights. Then while the rest, being but cowards, gave back a little, he shut to and bolted the doors against them, and sprang from the window on to the sea-washed rocks below. There he lay as one dead, until his squire, Gouvernail, coming in a little boat, took up his master, dressed his wounds, and carried him to the coast of England.

So Sir Tristram was minded to remain in that country for a time. Then, one day, as he rode through the forest near Camelot, there came running to him a fair lady who cried: "Sir Tristram, I claim your aid for the truest knight in all the world, and that is none other than King Arthur." "With a good heart," said Sir Tristram; "but where may I find him?" "Follow me," said the lady, who was none other than the Lady of the Lake herself, and ever mindful of the welfare of King Arthur. So he rode after her till he came to a castle, and in front of it he saw two knights who beset at once another knight, and when Sir Tristram came to the spot, the two had borne King Arthur to the ground and were about to cut off his head. Then Sir Tristram called to them to leave their traitor's work and look to themselves; with the word, one he pierced through with his spear and the other he cut down, and setting King Arthur again upon his horse, he rode with him until they met with certain of Arthur's knights. But when King Arthur would know his name, Tristram would give none, but said only that he was a poor errant knight; and so they parted.

But Arthur, when he was come back to Camelot, sent for Sir Launcelot and other of his knights, bidding them seek for such an one as was Sir Tristram and bring him to the court. So they departed, each his own way, and searched for many days, but in vain. Then it chanced, at last, as Sir Launcelot rode on his way, he espied Sir Tristram resting beside a tomb; and, as was the custom of knights errant, he called upon him to joust. So the two ran together and each broke his spear. Then they sprang to the ground and fought with their swords, and each thought that never had he encountered so stout or so skilled a knight. So fiercely they fought that, perforce, at last they must rest. Then said Sir Launcelot: "Fair Knight, I pray you tell me your name, for never have I met so good a knight." "In truth," said Sir Tristram, "I am loth to tell my name." "I marvel at that," said Sir Launcelot; "for mine I will tell you freely. I am Launcelot du Lac." Then was Sir Tristram filled at once with joy and with sorrow; with joy that at last he had encountered the noblest knight of the Round Table, with sorrow that he had done him such hurt, and without more ado he revealed his name. Now Sir Launcelot, who ever delighted in the fame of another, had long desired to meet Sir Tristram de Liones, and rejoicing to have found him, he knelt right courteously and proffered him his sword, as if he would yield to him. But Tristram would not have it so, declaring that, rather, he should yield to Sir Launcelot. So they embraced right heartily, and when Sir Launcelot questioned him, Sir Tristram acknowledged that it was he who had come to King Arthur's aid. Together, then, they rode to Camelot, and there Sir Tristram was received with great honour by King Arthur, who made him Knight of the Round Table.

Presently, to Tristram at Camelot, there came word that King Mark had driven the Fair Isolt from court, and compelled her to have her dwelling in a hut set apart for lepers. Then Sir Tristram was wroth indeed, and mounting his horse, rode forth that same hour, and rested not till he had found the lepers' hut, whence he bore the Queen to the castle known as the Joyous Garde; and there he held her, in safety and honour, in spite of all that King Mark could do. And all men honoured Sir Tristram, and felt sorrow for the Fair Isolt; while as for King Mark, they scorned him even more than before.

But to Sir Tristram, it was grief to be at enmity with his uncle who had made him knight, and at last he craved King Arthur's aid to reconcile him to Mark. So then the King, who loved Sir Tristram, sent messengers to

Cornwall to Mark, bidding him come forthwith to Camelot; and when the Cornish King was arrived, Arthur required him to set aside his enmity to Tristram, who had in all things been his loyal nephew and knight. And King Mark, his head full of hate, but fearful of offending his lord, King Arthur, made fair proffers of friendship, begging Sir Tristram to return to Cornwall with him, and promising to hold him in love and honour. So they were reconciled, and when King Mark returned to Cornwall, thither Sir Tristram escorted the Fair Isolt, and himself abode there, believing his uncle to mean truly and honourably by him.

But under a seeming fair exterior, King Mark hated Sir Tristram more than ever, and waited only to have him at an advantage. At length he contrived the opportunity he sought. For he hid him in the Queen's chamber at a time when he knew Sir Tristram would come there unarmed, to harp to the Fair Isolt the music that she loved. So as Sir Tristram, all unsuspecting, bent over his harp, Mark leaped from his lurking place and dealt him such a blow from behind that, on the instant, he fell dead at the feet of the Fair Isolt. So perished the good knight, Sir Tristram de Liones Nor did the Fair Isolt long survive him, for refusing all comfort, she pined away, and died within a few days, and was laid in a tomb beside that of her true knight. But the felon King paid the price of his treachery with his life; for Sir Launcelot himself avenged the death of his friend and the wrongs of the Fair Isolt.

BOOK IV
KING ARTHUR'S NEPHEWS

CHAPTER XVII
SIR GAWAIN AND THE LADY

Among the knights at King Arthur's court were his nephews, the sons of his sister, Queen Bellicent, and of that King Lot of Orkney, who had joined the league against Arthur in the first years of his reign.

Of each, many tales are told; of Sir Gawain and Sir Gareth to their great renown, but of Sir Mordred to his shame. For Sir Gawain and Sir Gareth were knights of great prowess; but Sir Mordred was a coward and a traitor, envious of other men's fame, and a tale-bearer.

Now Sir Gawain was known as the Ladies' Knight, and this is how he came by the name. It was at Arthur's marriage-feast, when Gawain had just been made knight, that a strange thing befell. There entered the hall a white hart, chased by a hound, and when it had run round the hall, it fled through the doorway again, still followed by the hound. Then, by Merlin's advice, the quest of the hart was given to Gawain as a new-made knight, to follow it and see what adventures it would bring him. So Sir Gawain rode away, taking with him three couples of greyhounds for the pursuit. At the last, the hounds caught the hart, and killed it just as it reached the court-yard of a castle. Then there came forth from the castle a knight, and he was grieved and wroth to see the hart slain, for it was given him by his lady; so, in his anger, he killed two of the hounds. At that moment Sir Gawain entered the court-yard, and an angry man was he when he saw his greyhounds slain. "Sir Knight," said he, "ye would have done better to have taken your vengeance on me rather than on dumb animals which but acted after their kind." "I will be avenged on you also," cried the knight; and the two rushed together, cutting and thrusting that it was wonderful they might so long endure. But at the last the knight grew faint, and crying for mercy, offered to yield to Sir Gawain. "Ye had no mercy on my hounds," said Sir Gawain. "I will make you all the amends in my power," answered the knight. But Sir Gawain would not be turned from his purpose, and unlacing the vanquished knight's helmet, was about to cut off his head, when a lady rushed out from the castle and flung herself on the body of the fallen knight. So it chanced that Sir Gawain's sword descending smote off the lady's head. Then was Sir Gawain grieved and sore ashamed for what he had done, and said to the knight: "I repent for what I have done; and here I give you your life. Go only to Camelot, to King Arthur's court, and tell him ye are sent by the knight who follows the quest of the white hart." "Ye have slain my lady," said the other, "and now I care not what befalls me." So he arose and went to King Arthur's court.

Then Sir Gawain prepared to rest him there for the night; but scarcely had he lain down when there fell upon him four knights, crying: "New-made knight, ye have shamed your knighthood, for a knight without mercy is without honour." Then was Sir Gawain borne to the earth, and would have been slain, but that there came forth from the castle four ladies who besought the knights to spare his life; so they consented and bound him prisoner.

The next morning Sir Gawain was brought again before the knights and their dames; and because he was King Arthur's nephew, the ladies desired that he should be set free, only they required that he should ride again to Camelot, the murdered lady's head hanging from his neck, and her dead body across his saddle-bow; and that when he arrived at the court he should confess his misdeeds.

So Sir Gawain rode sadly back to Camelot, and when he had told his tale, King Arthur was sore displeased. And Queen Guenevere held a court of her ladies to pass sentence on Sir Gawain for his ungentleness. These then decreed that, his life long, he must never refuse to fight for any lady who desired his services, and that ever he should be gentle and courteous and show mercy to all. From that time forth, Sir Gawain never failed in aught that dame or damsel asked of him, and so he won and kept the title of the Ladies' Knight.

CHAPTER XVIII
THE ADVENTURES OF SIR GARETH

Gareth was the youngest of the sons of Lot and Bellicent, and had grown up long after Gawain and Mordred left their home for King Arthur's court; so that when he came before the King, all humbly attired, he was known not even by his own brothers.

King Arthur was keeping Pentecost at Kink Kenadon on the Welsh border and, as his custom was, waited to begin the feast until some adventure should befall. Presently there was seen approaching a youth, who, to the wonderment of all that saw, leaned upon the shoulders of two men, his companions; and yet as he passed up the hall, he seemed a goodly youth, tall and broad-shouldered. When he stood before the King, suddenly he drew himself up, and after due greeting, said: "Sir King, I would ask of you three boons; one to be granted now and two hereafter when I shall require them." And Arthur, looking upon him, was pleased, for his countenance was open and honest. So he made answer; "Fair son, ask of me aught that is honourable and I will grant it." Then the youth said: "For this present, I ask only that ye will give me meat and drink for a year and a day." "Ye might have asked and had a better gift," replied the King; "tell me now your name." "At this time, I may not tell it," said the youth. Now King Arthur trusted every man until he proved himself unworthy, and in this youth he thought he saw one who should do nobly and win renown; so laughing, he bade him keep his own counsel since so he would, and gave him in charge to Sir Kay, the Seneschal.

Now Sir Kay was but harsh to those whom he liked not, and from the first he scorned the young man; "For none," said he, "but a low-born lout would crave meat and drink when he might have asked for a horse and arms." But Sir Launcelot and Sir Gawain took the youth's part. Neither knew him for Gareth of the Orkneys, but both believed him to be a youth of good promise who, for his own reasons, would pass in disguise for a season.

So Gareth lived the year among the kitchen-boys, all the time mocked and scorned by Sir Kay, who called him Fairhands because his hands were white and shapely. But Launcelot and Gawain showed him all courtesy, and failed not to observe how, in all trials of strength, he excelled his comrades, and that he was ever present to witness the feats of the knights in the tournaments.

So the year passed, and again King Arthur was keeping the feast of Pentecost with his knights, when a damsel entered the hall and asked his aid: "For," said she, "my sister is closely besieged in her castle by a strong knight who lays waste all her lands. And since I know that the knights of your court be the most renowned in the world, I have come to crave help of your mightiest." "What is your sister's name, and who is he that oppresses her?" asked the King. "The Red Knight, he is called," replied the damsel. "As for my sister I will not say her name, only that she is a high-born lady and owns broad lands." Then the King frowned and said: "Ye would have aid but will say no name. I may not ask knight of mine to go on such an errand."

Then forth stepped Gareth from among the serving men at the hall end and said: "Sir King, I have eaten of your meat in your kitchen this twelvemonth since, and now I crave my other two boons." "Ask and have," replied the King. "Grant me then the adventure of this damsel, and bid Sir Launcelot ride after me to knight me at my desire, for of him alone would I be made knight." "It shall be so," answered the King. "What!" cried the damsel, "I ask for a knight and ye give me a kitchen-boy. Shame on you, Sir King." And in great wrath she fled from the hall, mounted her palfrey and rode away. Gareth but waited to array himself in the armour which he had kept ever in readiness for the time when he should need it, and mounting his horse, rode after the damsel.

But when Sir Kay knew what had happened, he was wroth, and got to horse to ride after Gareth and bring him back. Even as Gareth overtook the damsel, so did Kay come up with him and cried: "Turn back, Fairhands! What, sir, do ye not know me?" "Yes," answered Gareth, "I know you for the most discourteous knight in Arthur's court." Then Sir Kay rode upon him with his lance, but Gareth turned it aside with his sword and pierced Sir Kay through the side so that he fell to the ground and lay there without motion. So Gareth took Sir Kay's shield and spear and was about to ride away, when seeing Sir Launcelot draw near, he called upon him to joust. At the first encounter, Sir Launcelot unhorsed Gareth, but quickly helped him to his feet. Then, at Gareth's desire, they fought together with swords, and Gareth did knightly till, at length, Sir Launcelot said, laughing: "Why should we fight any longer? Of a truth ye are a stout knight." "If that is indeed your thought, I pray you make me knight," cried Gareth. So Sir Launcelot knighted Gareth, who, bidding him farewell, hastened after the damsel, for she had ridden on again while the two knights talked. When she saw him coming, she cried: "Keep off! ye smell of the kitchen!" "Damsel," said Sir Gareth, "I must follow until I have fulfilled the adventure." "Till ye accomplish the adventure, Turn-spit? Your part in it shall soon be ended." "I can only do my best," answered Sir Gareth.

Now as they rode through the forest, they met with a knight sore beset by six thieves, and him Sir Gareth rescued. The knight then bade Gareth and the damsel rest at his castle, and entertained them right gladly until the morn, when the two rode forth again. Presently, they drew near to a deep river where two knights kept the ford. "How now, kitchen-knave? Will ye fight or escape while ye may?" cried the damsel. "I would fight though there were six instead of two," replied Sir Gareth. Therewith he encountered the one knight in mid-stream and struck him such a blow on the head that he fell, stunned, into the water and was drowned. Then, gaining the land, Gareth cleft in two both helmet and head of the other knight, and turned to the damsel, saying: "Lead on; I follow."

But the damsel mocked him, saying: "What a mischance is this that a kitchen-boy should slay two noble knights! Be not over-proud, Turn-spit. It was but luck, if indeed ye did not attack one knight from behind." "Say what you will, I follow," said Sir Gareth.

So they rode on again, the damsel in front and Sir Gareth behind, till they reached a wide meadow where stood many fair pavilions; and one, the largest, was all of blue, and the men who stood about it were clothed in blue, and bore shields and spears of that colour; and of blue, too, were the trappings of the horses. Then said the damsel: "Yonder is the Blue Knight, the goodliest that ever ye have looked upon, and five hundred knights own him lord." "I will encounter him," said Sir Gareth; "for if he be good knight and true as ye say, he will scarce set on me with all his following; and man to man, I fear him not." "Fie!" said the damsel, "for a dirty knave, ye brag loud. And even if ye overcome him, his might is as nothing to that of the Red Knight who besieges my lady sister. So get ye gone while ye may." "Damsel," said Sir Gareth, "ye are but ungentle so to rebuke me; for, knight or knave, I have done you good service, nor will I leave this quest while life is mine." Then the damsel was ashamed, and, looking curiously at Gareth, she said: "I would gladly know what manner of man ye are. For I heard you call yourself kitchen-knave before Arthur's self, but ye have ever answered patiently though I have chidden you shamefully; and courtesy comes only of gentle blood." Thereat Sir Gareth but laughed, and said: "He is no knight whom a maiden can anger by harsh words."

So talking, they entered the field, and there came to Sir Gareth a messenger from the Blue Knight to ask him if he came in peace or in war. "As your lord pleases," said Sir Gareth. So when the messenger had brought back this word, the Blue Knight mounted his horse, took his spear in his hand, and rode upon Sir Gareth. At their first encounter their lances shivered to pieces, and such was the shock that their horses fell dead. So they rushed on each other with sword and shield, cutting and slashing till the armour was hacked from their bodies; but at last, Sir Gareth smote the Blue Knight to the earth. Then the Blue Knight yielded, and at the damsel's entreaty, Sir Gareth spared his life.

So they were reconciled, and at the request of the Blue Knight, Sir Gareth and the damsel abode that night in his tents. As they sat at table, the Blue Knight said: "Fair damsel, are ye not called Linet?" "Yes," answered she, "and I am taking this noble knight to the relief of my sister, the Lady Liones." "God speed you, Sir," said the Blue Knight, "for he is a stout knight whom ye must meet. Long ago might he have taken the lady, but that he hoped that Sir Launcelot or some other of Arthur's most famous knights, coming to her rescue, might fall beneath his lance. If ye overthrow him, then are ye the peer of Sir Launcelot and Sir Tristram." "Sir Knight," answered Gareth, "I can but strive to bear me worthily as one whom the great Sir Launcelot made knight."

So in the morning they bade farewell to the Blue Knight, who vowed to carry to King Arthur word of all that Gareth had achieved; and they rode on, till, in the evening, they came to a little ruined hermitage where there awaited them a dwarf, sent by the Lady Liones, with all manner of meats and other store. In the morning, the dwarf set out again to bear word to his lady that her rescuer was come. As he drew near the castle, the Red Knight stopped him, demanding whence he came. "Sir," said the dwarf, "I have been with my lady's sister, who brings with her a knight to the rescue of my lady." "It is lost labour," said the Red Knight; "even though she brought Launcelot or Tristram, I hold myself a match for them." "He is none of these," said the dwarf, "but he has overthrown the knights who kept the ford, and the Blue Knight yielded to him." "Let him come," said the Red Knight; "I shall soon make an end of him, and a shameful death shall he have at my hands, as many a better knight has had." So saying, he let the dwarf go.

Presently, there came riding towards the castle Sir Gareth and the damsel Linet, and Gareth marvelled to see hang from the trees some forty knights in goodly armour, their shields reversed beside them. And when he inquired of the damsel, she told him how these were the bodies of brave knights who, coming to the rescue of the Lady Liones, had been overthrown and shamefully done to death by the Red Knight. Then was Gareth shamed and angry, and he vowed to make an end of these evil practices. So at last they drew near to the castle walls, and saw how the plain around was covered with the Red Knight's tents, and the noise was that of a great army. Hard by was a tall sycamore tree, and from it hung a mighty horn, made of an elephant's tusk. Spurring his horse, Gareth rode to it, and blew such a blast that those on the castle walls heard it; the knights came forth from their tents to see who blew so bold a blast, and from a window of the castle the Lady Liones looked forth and waved her hand to her champion. Then, as Sir Gareth made his reverence to the lady, the Red Knight called roughly to him to leave his courtesy and look to himself; "For," said he, "she is mine, and to have her, I have fought many a battle." "It is but vain labour," said Sir Gareth, "since she loves you not. Know, too, Sir Knight, that I have vowed to rescue her from you." "So did many another who now hangs on a tree," replied the Red Knight, "and soon ye shall hang beside them." Then both laid their spears in rest, and spurred their horses. At the first encounter, each smote the other full in the shield, and the girths of the saddles bursting, they were borne to the earth, where they lay for awhile as if dead. But presently they rose, and setting their shields before them, rushed upon each other with their swords, cutting and hacking till the armour lay on the ground in fragments. So they fought till noon and then rested; but soon they renewed the battle, and so furiously they fought, that often they fell to the ground together. Then, when the bells sounded for evensong, the knights rested again a while, unlacing their helms to breathe the evening air. But looking up to the castle windows, Gareth saw the Lady Liones gazing earnestly upon him; then he caught up his helmet, and calling to the Red Knight, bade him make ready for the battle; "And this time," said he, "we will make an end of it." "So be it," said the Red Knight. Then the Red Knight smote Gareth on the hand that his sword flew from his grasp, and with another blow he brought him grovelling to the earth. At the sight of this, Linet cried aloud, and hearing her, Gareth, with a mighty effort, threw off the Red Knight, leaped to his sword and got it again within his hand. Then he pressed the Red Knight harder than ever, and at the last bore him to the earth, and unlacing his helm, made ready to slay him; but the Red Knight cried aloud: "Mercy; I yield." At first, remembering the evil deaths of the forty good knights, Gareth was unwilling to spare him; but the Red Knight besought him to have mercy, telling him how, against his will, he had been bound by a vow to make war on Arthur's knights. So Sir Gareth relented, and bade him set forth at once for Kink Kenadon and entreat the King's pardon for his evil past. And this the Red Knight promised to do.

Then amidst much rejoicing, Sir Gareth was borne into the castle. There his wounds were dressed by the Lady Liones, and there he rested until he recovered his strength. And having won her love, when Gareth returned to Arthur's court, the Lady Liones rode with him, and they two were wed with great pomp in the presence of the whole Fellowship of the Round Table; the King rejoicing much that his nephew had done so valiantly. So Sir Gareth lived happily with Dame Liones, winning fame and the love of all true knights. As for Linet, she came again to Arthur's court and wedded Sir Gareth's younger brother, Sir Gaheris.

BOOK V
SIR GERAINT

CHAPTER XIX
THE ADVENTURES OF GERAINT

It befell, one Whitsunday, that Arthur was holding his court at Caerleon, when word was brought to him of a splendid white stag that ranged the Forest of Dean, and forthwith the King proclaimed a hunt for the morrow.

So, with the dawn, there was much trampling of hoofs and baying of hounds as all the knights got to horse; but Queen Guenevere herself, though she had said she would ride with the hunt, slept late, and when she called her maidens to her, it was broad day. Then, with much haste, she arrayed herself, and taking one of her ladies with her, rode to a little rising ground in the forest, near which, as she well knew, the hunt must pass.

Presently, as she waited, there came riding by the gallant knight, Geraint of Devon. He was arrayed neither for the chase nor for the fight, but wore a surcoat of white satin and about him a loose scarf of purple, with a golden apple at each corner. And when the Queen had answered his salutation, she said: "How is it, Prince, that ye be not ridden with the hunters?" "Madam," answered he, "with shame I say it; I slept too late." Smiling, the Queen said: "Then are we both in the same case, for I also arose too late. But tarry with me, and soon ye will hear the baying of the hounds; for often I have known them break covert here."

Then as they waited on the little woodland knoll, there came riding past a knight full armed, a lady with him, and behind them a dwarf, misshapen and evil-looking, and they passed without word or salutation to the Queen.

Then said Guenevere to Geraint: "Prince, know ye yonder knight?" "Nay, madam," said he; "his arms I know not, and his face I might not see." Thereupon the Queen turned to her attendant and said: "Ride after them quickly and ask the dwarf his master's name." So the maiden did as she was bidden; but when she inquired of the dwarf, he answered her roughly: "I will not tell thee my master's name." "Since thou art so churlish," said she,

"I will even ask him himself." "That thou shalt not," he cried, and struck her across the face with his whip. So the maiden, alarmed and angered, rode back to the Queen and told her all that had happened. "Madam," cried Geraint, "the churl has wronged your maiden and insulted your person. I pray you, suffer me to do your errand myself." With the word, he put spurs to his horse and rode after the three. And when he had come up with the dwarf, he asked the knight's name as the maiden had done, and the dwarf answered him as he had answered the Queen's lady. "I will speak with thy master himself," said Geraint. "Thou shalt not, by my faith!" said the dwarf. "Thou art not honourable enough to speak with my lord." "I have spoken with men of as good rank as he," answered Geraint, and would have turned his horse's head that he might ride after the knight; but the dwarf struck him across the face such a blow that the blood spurted forth over his purple scarf. Then, in his wrath, Geraint clapped hand to sword, and would have slain the churl, but that he bethought him how powerless was such a misshapen thing. So refraining himself, he rode back to the Queen and said: "Madam, for the time the knight has escaped me. But, with your leave, I will ride after him, and require of him satisfaction for the wrong done to yourself and to your maiden. It must be that I shall come presently to a town where I may obtain armour. Farewell; if I live, ye shall have tidings of me by next even." "Farewell," said the Queen; "I shall ever hold your good service in remembrance."

So Geraint rode forth on his quest, and followed the road to the ford of the Usk, where he crossed, and then went on his way until he came to a town, at the further end of which rose a mighty castle. And as he entered the town, he saw the knight and the lady, and how, as they rode through the streets, from every window the folk craned their necks to see them pass, until they entered the castle and the gate fell behind them. Then was Geraint satisfied that they would not pass thence that night, and turned him about to see where he could obtain the use of arms that, the next day, he might call the knight to account.

Now it seemed that the whole town was in a ferment. In every house, men were busy polishing shields, sharpening swords, and washing armour, and scarce could they find time to answer questions put to them; so at the last, finding nowhere in the town to rest, Geraint rode in the direction of a ruined palace, which stood a little apart from the town, and was reached by a marble bridge spanning a deep ravine. Seated on the bridge was an old man, hoary-headed, and clothed in the tattered remains of what had once been splendid attire, who gave Geraint courteous greeting. "Sir," said Geraint, "I pray you, know ye where I may find shelter for this night?" "Come with me," said the old man, "and ye shall have the best my old halls afford." So saying, he led Geraint into a great stone-paved court-yard, surrounded by buildings, once strong fortifications, but then half burned and ruinous. There he bade Geraint dismount, and led the way into an upper chamber, where sat an aged dame, and with her a maiden the fairest that ever Geraint had looked upon, for all that her attire was but a faded robe and veil. Then the old man spoke to the maiden, saying: "Enid, take the good knight's charger to a stall and give him corn. Then go to the town and buy us provision for a feast to-night." Now it pleased not Geraint that the maiden should thus do him service; but when he made to accompany her, the old man, her father, stayed him and kept him in converse until presently she was returned from the town and had made all ready for the evening meal. Then they sat them down to supper, the old man and his wife with Geraint between them; and the fair maid, Enid, waited upon them, though it irked the Prince to see her do such menial service.

So as they ate, they talked, and presently Geraint asked of the cause why the palace was all in ruins. "Sir knight," said the old man, "I am Yniol, and once I was lord of a broad earldom. But my nephew, whose guardian I had been, made war upon me, affirming that I had withheld from him his dues; and being the stronger, he prevailed, and seized my lands and burnt my halls, even as ye see. For the townsfolk hold with him, because that, with his tournaments and feastings, he brings many strangers their way." "What then is all the stir in the town even now?" asked Geraint. "To-morrow," said the Earl, "they hold the tournament of the Sparrow-Hawk. In the midst of the meadow are set up two forks, and on the forks a silver rod, and on the rod the form of a Sparrow-Hawk. Two years has it been won by the stout knight Edeyrn, and if he win it the morrow, it shall be his for aye, and he himself known as the Sparrow-Hawk." "Tell me," cried Geraint, "is that the knight that rode this day with a lady and a dwarf to the castle hard by?" "The same," said Yniol; "and a bold knight he is." Then Geraint told them of the insult offered that morning to Queen Guenevere and her maiden, and how he had ridden forth to obtain satisfaction. "And now, I pray you," said Geraint, "help me to come by some arms, and in to-morrow's lists will I call this Sparrow-Hawk to account." "Arms have I," answered the Earl, "old and rusty indeed, yet at your service. But, Sir Knight, ye may not appear in to-morrow's tournament, for none may contend unless he bring with him a lady in whose honour he jousts." Then cried Geraint: "Lord Earl, suffer me to lay lance in rest in honour of the fair maiden, your daughter. And if I fall to-morrow, no harm shall have been done her, and if I win, I will love her my life long, and make her my true wife." Now Enid, her service ended, had left them to their talk; but the Earl, rejoicing that so noble a knight should seek his daughter's love, promised that, with the maiden's consent, all should be as the Prince desired.

So they retired to rest that night, and the next day at dawn, Geraint arose, and, donning the rusty old armour lent him by Earl Yniol, rode to the lists; and there amongst the humbler sort of onlookers, he found the old Earl and his wife and with them their fair daughter.

Then the heralds blew their trumpets, and Edeyrn bade his lady-love take the Sparrow-Hawk, her due as fairest of the fair. "Forbear," cried Geraint; "here is one fairer and nobler for whom I claim the prize of the tournament." "Do battle for it, then!" cried Edeyrn. So the two took their lances and rushed upon one another with a crash like thunder, and each broke his spear. Thus they encountered once and again; but at the last Geraint bore down upon Edeyrn with such force that he carried him from his horse, saddle and all. Then he dismounted, and the two rushed upon each other with their swords. Long they fought, the sparks flying and their breath coming hard, till, exerting all his strength, Geraint dealt the other such a blow as cleft his helmet and bit to the bone. Then Edeyrn flung away his sword and yielded him. "Thou shalt have thy life," said Geraint, "upon condition that, forthwith, thou goest to Arthur's court, there to deliver thyself to our Queen, and make such atonement as shall be adjudged thee, for the insult offered her yester morn." "I will do so," answered Edeyrn; and when his wounds had been dressed he got heavily to horse and rode forth to Caerleon.

Then the young Earl, Yniol's nephew, adjudged the Sparrow-Hawk to Geraint, as victor in the tourney, and prayed him to come to his castle to rest and feast. But Geraint, declining courteously, said that it behoved him to go there where he had rested the night before. "Where may that have been?" asked the Earl; "for though ye come not to my castle, yet would I see that ye fare as befits your valour." "I rested even with Yniol, your uncle," answered Geraint. The young Earl mused awhile, and then he said: "I will seek you, then, in my uncle's halls, and bring with me the means to furnish forth a feast."

And so it was. Scarcely had Prince Geraint returned to the ruined hall and bathed and rested him after his labours, when the young Earl arrived, and with him forty of his followers bearing all manner of stores and plenishings. And that same hour, the young Earl was accorded with Yniol, his uncle, restoring to him the lands of which he had deprived him, and pledging his word to build up again the ruined palace.

When they had gone to the banquet, then came to them Enid, attired in beautiful raiment befitting her rank; and the old Earl led her to Geraint, saying: "Prince, here is the maiden for whom ye fought, and freely I bestow her upon you." So Geraint took her hand before them all and said: "She shall ride with me to Caerleon, and there will I wed her before Arthur's court." Then to Enid he said: "Gentle maiden, bear with me when I pray you to don the faded robe and veil in which first I saw you." And Enid, who was ever gentle and meek, did as he desired, and that evening they rode to Caerleon.

So when they drew near the King's palace, word was brought to Guenevere of their approach. Then the Queen went forth to greet the good knight, and when she had heard all his story, she kissed the maiden, and leading her into her own chamber, arrayed her right royally for her marriage with the Prince. And that evening they were wed amidst great rejoicing, in the presence of all the knights and ladies of the court, the King himself giving Enid to her husband. Many happy days they spent at Caerleon, rejoicing in the love and good-will of Arthur and his Queen.

CHAPTER XX
GERAINT AND ENID

Geraint and the fair Enid abode more than a year at Arthur's court; Enid winning daily more and more the love of all by her gentleness and goodness, and Geraint being ever amongst the foremost in the tournament. But presently there came word of robber raids upon the borders of Devon; wherefore the Prince craved leave of Arthur to return to his own land, there to put down wrong and oppression, and maintain order and justice. And the King bade him go and secure to every man his due.

So Geraint passed to his own land, Enid going with him; and soon he had driven the oppressors from their strongholds and established peace and order, so that the poor man dwelt in his little cot secure in his possessions. But when all was done, and there was none dared defy him, Geraint abode at home, neglectful of the tournament and the chase, and all those manly exercises in which he had once excelled, content if he had but the companionship of his wife; so that his nobles murmured because he withdrew himself from their society, and the common people jeered at him for a laggard.

Now these evil rumours came to Enid's ears, and it grieved her that she should be the cause, however unwillingly, of her husband's dishonour; and since she could not bring herself to speak to her lord of what was in her heart, daily she grew more sorrowful, till the Prince, aware of her altered demeanour, became uneasy, not knowing its source.

So time went by till it chanced, one summer morning, that with the first rays of the sun, Enid awoke from her slumbers, and, rising, gazed upon her husband as he lay, and marvelled at his strength. "Alas!" said she, "to be the cause that my lord suffers shame! Surely I should find courage to tell him all, were I indeed true wife to him!" Then, by ill chance, her tears falling upon him awoke him, so that he heard her words, but brokenly, and seeing her weep and hearing her accuse herself, it came into his thought that, for all his love and care for her, she was weary of him, nay, even that perhaps she loved him not at all. In anger and grief he called to his squire and bade him saddle his charger and a palfrey for Enid; and to her he said: "Put on thy meanest attire, and thou shalt ride with me into the wilderness. It seems that I have yet to win me fame; but before thou seest home again, thou shalt learn if indeed I am fallen so low as thou deemest." And Enid, wondering and troubled, answered, "I know naught of thy meaning, my lord." "Ask me nothing," said Geraint. So sorrowfully and in silence Enid arrayed herself, choosing for her apparel the faded robe and veil in which first her lord had seen her.

Then the squire brought them their horses; but when he would have mounted and ridden after, Geraint forbade him. And to Enid the Prince said: "Ride before me and turn not back, no matter what thou seest or hearest. And unless I speak to thee, say not a word to me."

So they rode forward along the least frequented road till they came to a vast forest, which they entered. There Enid, as she rode in front, saw four armed men lurking by the road, and one said to the other: "See, now is our opportunity to win much spoil at little cost; for we may easily overcome this doleful knight, and take from him his arms and lady." And Enid hearing them, was filled with fear and doubt; for she longed to warn her lord of his danger, yet feared to arouse his wrath, seeing he had bidden her keep silence. Then said she to herself: "Better to anger him, even to the slaying of me, than have the misery of seeing him perish." So she waited till Geraint drew near, and said: "Lord, there lie in wait for thee four men fully armed, to slay and rob thee." Then he answered her in anger: "Did I desire thy silence or thy warning? Look, then, and whether thou desirest my life or my death, thou shalt see that I dread not these robbers." Then, as the foremost of the four rode upon him, Geraint drove upon him with his spear with such force that the weapon stood out a cubit behind him; and so he did with the second, and the third, and the fourth. Then, dismounting from his horse, he stripped the dead felons of their armour, bound it upon their horses, and tying the bridle reins together, bade Enid drive the beasts before her. "And," said he, "I charge thee, at thy peril, speak no word to me."

So they went forward; and presently Enid saw how three horsemen, well armed and well mounted, rode towards them. And one said to the other: "Good fortune, indeed! Here are four horses and four suits of armour for us, and but one knight to deal with; a craven too, by the way he hangs his head." Then Enid thought within herself how her lord was wearied with his former combat, and resolved to warn him even at her own peril. So she waited till he was come up with her, and said: "Lord, there be three men riding towards us, and they promise themselves rich booty at small cost." Wrathfully spoke Geraint: "Their words anger me less than thy disobedience"; and immediately rushing upon the mid-most of the three knights, he bore him from his horse; then he turned upon the other two who rode against him at the same moment, and slew them both. As with the former caitiffs, so now Geraint stripped the three of their armour, bound it upon the horses, and bade Enid drive these forward with the other four.

Again they rode on their way, and, for all his anger, it smote Geraint to the heart to see the gentle lady labouring to drive forward the seven horses. So he bade her stay, for they would go no farther then, but rest that night as best they might in the forest; and scarcely had they dismounted and tethered the horses before Geraint, wearied with his encounters, fell asleep; but Enid remained watching, lest harm should come to her lord while he slept.

With the first ray of light, Geraint awoke, and his anger against Enid was not passed; so, without more ado, he set her on her palfrey and bade her drive the horses on in front as before, charging her that, whatever befell, that day at least, she should keep silence.

Soon they passed from the forest into open land, and came upon a river flowing through broad meadows where the mowers toiled. Then, as they waited to let the horses drink their fill, there drew near a youth, bearing a basket of bread and meat and a blue pitcher covered over with a bowl. So when the youth saluted them, Geraint stayed him, asking whence he came. "My lord," said the lad, "I am come from the town hard by, to bring the mowers their breakfast." "I pray thee, then," said the Prince, "give of the food to this lady, for she is faint." "That will I gladly," answered the youth, "and do ye also partake, noble sir"; and he spread the meal for them on the grass while they dismounted. So when they had eaten and were refreshed, the youth gathered up the basket and pitcher, saying he would return to the town for food for the mowers. "Do so," said the Prince, "and when thou art come there, take for me the best lodging that thou mayst. And for thy fair service, take a horse and armour, whichsoever thou wilt." "My lord, ye reward me far beyond my deserts," cried the youth. "Right gladly will I make all ready against your arrival, and acquaint my master, the Earl, of your coming."

So Geraint and Enid followed after the youth to the town, and there they found everything prepared for their comfort, even as he had promised; for they were lodged in a goodly chamber well furnished with all that they might require. Then said Geraint to Enid: "Abide at one end of the room and I will remain at the other. And call the woman of the house if thou desirest her aid and comfort in aught." "I thank thee, lord," answered Enid patiently; but she called for no service, remaining silent and forlorn in the farthest corner of the great chamber.

Presently there came to the house the Earl, the youth's master, and with him twelve goodly knights to wait upon him. And Geraint welcomed them right heartily, bidding the host bring forth his best to furnish a feast. So they sat them down at the table, each in his degree according to his rank, and feasted long and merrily; but Enid remained the while shrinking into her corner if perchance she might escape all notice.

As they sat at the banquet, the Earl asked Prince Geraint what quest he followed. "None but mine own inclination and the adventure it may please heaven to send," said Geraint. Then the Earl, whose eye had oft sought Enid as she sat apart, said: "Have I your good leave to cross the room and speak to your fair damsel? For she joins us not in the feast." "Ye have it freely," answered the Prince. So the Earl arose, and approaching Enid, bowed before her, and spoke to her in low tones, saying: "Damsel, sad life is yours, I fear, to journey with yonder man." "To travel the road he takes is pleasant enough to me," answered Enid. "But see what slights he puts upon you! To suffer you to journey thus, unattended by page or maiden, argues but little love or reverence for you." "It is as nothing, so that I am with him," said Enid. "Nay, but," said the Earl, "see how much happier a life might be yours. Leave this churl, who values you not, and all that I have, land and riches, and my love and service for ever shall be yours." "Ye cannot tempt me, with aught that ye can offer, to be false to him to whom I vowed my faith," said she. "Ye are a fool!" said the Earl in a fierce whisper. "One word to these my knights, and yonder is a dead man. Then who shall hinder me that I take you by force? Nay, now, be better advised, and I vow you my whole devotion for all time." Then was Enid filled with dread of the man and his might, and seeking but to gain time, she said: "Suffer me to be for this present, my lord, and to-morrow ye shall come and take me as by force. Then shall my name not suffer loss." "So be it," said he; "I will not fail you." With that he left her, and taking his leave of Geraint, departed with his followers.

Never a word of what the Earl had said did Enid tell her husband that night; and on the departure of his guests, the Prince, unheedful of her, flung him on the couch, and soon slept, despite his grief and wrath. But Enid watched again that night, and, before cock-crow, arose, set all his armour ready in one place, and then, though fearful of his wrath, stepped to his side and touching him gently, said: "Awake, my lord, and arm you, and save me and yourself." Then she told him of all the Earl had said and of the device she had used to save them both. Then wrathfully he rose and armed himself, bidding her rouse the host to saddle and bring forth the horses. When all was ready, Prince Geraint asked the man his reckoning. "Ye owe but little," said the host. "Take then the seven horses and the suits of armour," said Geraint. "Why, noble sir," cried the host, "I scarce have spent the value of one." "The richer thou," answered Geraint. "Now show me the road from the town."

So the man guided them from the town, and scarce was he returned when Earl Durm — for so was the Earl named — hammered at the door, with forty followers at his back. "Where is the knight who was here erewhile?" "He is gone hence, my lord," answered the host. "Fool and villain!" cried the Earl, "why didst thou suffer him to escape? Which way went he?" And the man, fearful and trembling, directed the Earl the road Geraint had gone.

So it came to pass, as they rode on their way, Enid in front, the Prince behind, that it seemed to Enid she heard the beat of many horse-hoofs. And, as before, she broke Geraint's command, caring little for aught that might befall her in comparison of loss to him. "My lord," said she, "seest thou yonder knight pursuing thee and many another with him?" "Yea, in good truth, I see him," said Geraint, "and I see, too, that never wilt thou obey me." Then he turned him about and, laying lance in rest, bore straight down upon Earl Durm, who foremost rushed upon him; and such was the shock of their encounter, that Earl Durm was borne from his saddle and lay without motion as one dead. And Geraint charged fiercely upon the Earl's men, unhorsing some and wounding others; and the rest, having little heart for the fight after their master's overthrow, turned and fled.

Then Geraint signed to Enid to ride on as before, and so they journeyed the space of another hour while the summer sun beat upon them with ever increasing force. Now the Prince had received a grievous hurt in the encounter with Earl Durm and his men; but such was his spirit that he heeded it not, though the wound bled sore under his armour. Presently, as they rode, there came to them the sound of wailing, and by the wayside they saw a lady weeping bitterly over a knight who lay dead on the ground. "Lady," said Geraint, "what has befallen you?" "Noble knight," she replied, "as we rode through the forest, my husband and I, three villains set upon him at once, and slew him." "Which way went they?" asked Geraint. "Straight on by this high-road that ye follow even now," answered she. Then Geraint bade Enid remain with the lady while he rode on to take vengeance on the miscreants. And Enid waited fearfully the long while he was gone, and her heart rejoiced when she saw him returning. But soon her joy was turned to sorrow, for his armour was all dented and covered with blood and his face ghastly; and even as he reached her side, he fell from his horse, prone on the ground. Then Enid strove to loosen his armour, and having found the wound, she staunched it as best she might and bound it with her veil. And taking his head on her lap, she chafed his hands and tried with her own body to shield him from the sun, her tears falling fast the while. So she waited till, perchance, help might come that way; and presently, indeed, she heard the tramp of horses, and a troop came riding by with the Earl Limours at their head. And when the Earl saw the two fallen knights and the weeping women beside them, he stayed his horse, and said: "Ladies, what has chanced to you?" Then she whose husband had been slain said: "Sir, three caitiffs set on my husband at once and slew him. Then came this good knight and went in pursuit of them, and as I think, slew them; but when he came back, he fell from his horse, sore wounded as ye see, and, I fear me, by now he is dead." "Nay, gentle sir," cried Enid; "it cannot be that he is dead. Only, I beseech you, suffer two of your men to carry him hence to some place of shelter where he may have help and tendance." "I misdoubt me, it is but labour wasted," said the Earl; "nevertheless, for the sake of your fair face, it shall be as ye desire." Then he ordered two of his men to carry Geraint to his halls and two more to stay behind and bury the dead knight, while he caused the two women to be placed on led horses; and so they rode to his castle. When they were arrived there, the two spearmen who had carried Geraint, placed him on a settle in the hall, and Enid crouched by his side, striving if by any means she might bring him back to life. And gradually Geraint recovered, though still he lay as in a swoon, hearing indeed what passed around him, but dimly, as from a distance.

Soon there came into the hall many servitors, who brought forth the tables and set thereon all manner of meats, haunches of venison and boars' heads and great pasties, together with huge flagons of wine. Then when all was set, there came trooping to the board the whole company of Earl Limours' retainers; last of all came the Earl himself and took his place on the raised dais. Suddenly, as he feasted and made merry, he espied Enid, who, mistrusting him utterly, would fain have escaped his eye. And when he saw her, he cried: "Lady, cease wasting sorrow on a dead man and come hither. Thou shalt have a seat by my side; ay, and myself, too, and my Earldom to boot." "I thank you, lord," she answered meekly, "but, I pray you, suffer me to be as I am." "Thou art a fool," said Limours; "little enough he prized thee, I warrant, else had he not put thy beauty to such scorn, dressing it in faded rags! Nay, be wise; eat and drink, and thou wilt think the better of me and my fair proffer." "I will not," cried Enid; "I will neither eat nor drink, till my lord arise and eat with me." "Thou vowest more than thou canst perform. He is dead already. Nay, thou shalt drink." With the word, he strode to her and thrust into her hand a goblet brimming with wine, crying, "Drink." "Nay, lord," she said, "I beseech you, spare me and be pitiful." "Gentleness avails nothing with thee," cried the Earl in wrath; "thou hast scorned my fair courtesy. Thou shalt taste the contrary." So saying, he smote her across the face.

Then Enid, knowing all her helplessness, uttered an exceeding bitter cry, and the sound roused Geraint. Grasping his sword, with one bound he was upon the Earl and, with one blow, shore his neck in two. Then those who sat at meat fled shrieking, for they believed that the dead had come to life.

But Geraint gazed upon Enid and his heart smote him, thinking of the sorrow he had brought upon her. "Lady and sweet wife," he cried, "for the wrong I have done thee, pardon me. For, hearing thy words not three days since at morn, I doubted thy love and thy loyalty. But now I know thee and trust thee beyond the power of words to shake my faith." "Ah! my lord," cried Enid, "fly, lest they return and slay thee." "Knowest thou where is my charger?" "I will bring thee to it." So they found the war-horse and Geraint mounted it, setting Enid behind him; thus they went forth in the direction of the nearest town, that they might find rest and succour. Then, as they rode, there came forth from a glade of the forest a knight, who, seeing Geraint, at once laid lance in rest as if he would ride upon him. And Enid, fearing for her husband, shrieked aloud, crying: "Noble knight, whosoever ye be, encounter not with a man nigh wounded to the death." Immediately the knight raised his lance and looking more attentively upon, them, he exclaimed: "What! is it Prince Geraint? Pardon me, noble knight, that I knew you not at once. I am that Edeyrn whom once ye overthrew and spared. At Arthur's court, whither ye sent me, I was shown kindness and courtesy little deserved, and now am I knight of Arthur's Round Table. But how came ye in such a case?" Then Geraint told him of his encounter with the three caitiffs, and how he had afterwards been borne to the castle of Earl Limours. "To do justice on that same felon is Arthur himself here even now," cried Edeyrn. "His camp is hard by." Then Geraint told Edeyrn how Limours lay dead in his own halls, justly punished for the many wrongs he had done, and how his people were scattered. "Come then yourself to greet the King and tell him what has chanced." So he led the way to Arthur's camp, where it lay in the forest hard by. Then were they welcomed by the King himself and a tent assigned to them, where Geraint rested until his wounds were healed.

Never again, from that time forth, had Geraint a doubt of the love and truth of Enid; and never from that time had she to mourn that he seemed to set small store by his knightly fame. For after he was cured, they returned to their own land, and there Geraint upheld the King's justice, righting wrong and putting down robbery and oppression, so that the people blessed him and his gentle wife. Year by year, his fame grew, till his name was known through all lands; and at last, when his time was come, he died a knightly death, as he had lived a knightly life, in the service of his lord, King Arthur.

BOOK VI
THE LADY OF THE FOUNTAIN

CHAPTER XXI
THE LADY OF THE FOUNTAIN

King Arthur was holding his court at Caerleon-upon-Usk, and it was the time of the evening banquet, when there entered the hall the good knight, Sir Kynon. A brave warrior was he, and of good counsel, but he seemed in weary plight as, after due salutation to all, he took his place at the Round Table. So it was that all were eager to hear of his adventure, yet none would question him until he had eaten and drunk. But when he was refreshed, the King said to him: "Whence come ye, Sir Kynon? For it would seem that ye have met with hard adventure." "Sir King," answered Kynon, "it has been with me as never before; for I have encountered with, and been overthrown by, a single knight." All were filled with wonder at his words, for never before had Sir Kynon been worsted in any meeting, man to man. Then said the King: "The stoutest of us must some time meet his match; yet did ye bear you valiantly, I doubt not. Tell us now, I pray you, of your adventures." "Noble lord," said Kynon, "I had determined to journey into other lands; for I would seek new and untried adventures. So I passed into a far land, and it chanced, one day, that I found myself in the fairest valley I had ever seen. Through it there flowed a mighty river, which I followed, until I came, as evening fell, to a castle, the largest and strongest I have ever seen. At the castle gate I espied a man of right noble mien, who greeted me courteously, and bade me enter. So as we sat at supper, he inquired of my journey and the quest I followed, and I told him how I sought but adventure, and whether, perchance, I might encounter one stronger than myself. Then the lord of the castle smiled and said: 'I can bring you to such an one, if ye would rather that I showed you your disadvantage than your advantage.' And when I questioned him further, he replied: 'Sleep here this night, and to-morrow I will show you such an one as ye seek.' So I rested that night, and with the dawn I rose and took my leave of the lord of the castle, who said to me: 'If ye will persevere in your quest, follow the path to the head of the glade, and ascend the wooded steep until ye come to an open space in the forest, with but one great tree in its midst. Under the tree is a fountain, and beside it a marble slab to which is chained a silver bowl. Take a bowlful of water and dash it upon the slab, and presently there will appear a knight spurring to encounter with you. If ye flee, he will pursue, but if ye overcome him, there exists none in this world whom ye need fear to have ado with.'

"Forthwith I departed, and following these directions, I came at last to such a space as he described, with the tree and fountain in its midst. So I took the bowl and dashed water from the fountain upon the marble slab, and, on the instant, came a clap of thunder so loud as near deafened me, and a storm of hailstones the biggest that ever man saw. Scarce was I recovered from my confusion, when I saw a knight galloping towards me. All in black was he, and he rode a black horse. Not a word we spoke, but we dashed against each other, and at the first encounter I was unhorsed. Still not a word spoke the Black Knight, but passing the butt-end of his lance through my horse's reins, rode away, leaving me shamed and on foot. So I made my way back to the castle, and there I was entertained again that night right hospitably, none questioning me as to my adventure. The next morning, when I rose, there awaited me a noble steed, ready saddled and bridled, and I rode away and am returned hither. And now ye know my story and my shame."

Then were all grieved for the discomfiture of Sir Kynon, who had ever borne himself boldly and courteously to all; and they strove to console him as best they might. Presently there rose from his siege the good knight Sir Owain of Rheged, and said: "My lord, I pray you, give me leave to take upon me this adventure. For I would gladly seek this wondrous fountain and encounter with this same Black Knight." So the King consented, and on the morrow Sir Owain armed him, mounted his horse, and rode forth the way Sir Kynon had directed him.

So he journeyed many a day until at last he reached the valley of which Sir Kynon had told, and presently he came to the strong castle and, at the gate, met the lord thereof, even as Sir Kynon had done. And the lord of the castle gave him a hearty welcome and made him good cheer, asking nothing of his errand till they were seated about the board. Then, when questioned, Sir Owain declared his quest, that he sought the knight who guarded the fountain. So the lord of the castle, failing to dissuade Sir Owain from the adventure, directed him how he might find the forest glade wherein was the wondrous fountain.

With the dawn, Sir Owain rose, mounted his horse, and rode forward until he had found the fountain. Then he dashed water on the marble slab and instantly there burst over him the fearful hailstorm, and through it there came pricking towards him the Black Knight on the black steed. In the first onset, they broke their lances and then, drawing sword, they fought blade to blade. Sore was the contest, but at the last Owain dealt the Black Knight so fierce a blow that the sword cut through helmet and bone to the very brain. Then the Black Knight knew that he had got his death-wound, and turning his horse's head, fled as fast as he might, Sir Owain following close behind. So they came, fast galloping, to the gate of a mighty castle, and instantly the portcullis was raised and the Black Knight dashed through the gateway. But Sir Owain, following close behind, found himself a prisoner, fast caught between two gates; for as the Black Knight passed through the inner of the two gates, it was closed before Sir Owain could follow. For the moment none noticed Sir Owain, for all were busied about the Black Knight, who drew not rein till he was come to the castle hall; then as he strove to dismount, he fell from his saddle, dead.

All this Sir Owain saw through the bars of the gate that held him prisoner; and he judged that his time was come, for he doubted not but that the people of the castle would hold his life forfeit for the death of their lord. So as he waited, suddenly there stood at his side a fair damsel, who, laying finger on lip, motioned to him to follow her. Much wondering, he obeyed, and climbed after her up a dark winding staircase, that led from the gateway into a tiny chamber high in the tower. There she set food and wine before him, bidding him eat; then when he was refreshed, she asked him his name and whence he came. "Truly," answered he, "I am Owain of Rheged, knight of King Arthur's Round Table, who, in fair fight, have wounded, I doubt not to the death, the Black Knight that guards the fountain and, as I suppose, the lord of this castle. Wherefore, maiden, if ye intend me evil, lead me where I may answer for my deed, boldly, man to man." "Nay," answered the damsel eagerly, "in a good hour ye are come. Well I know your name, for even here have we heard of your mighty deeds; and by good fortune it may be that ye shall release my lady." "Who is your lady?" asked Sir Owain. "None other than the rightful Chatelaine of this castle and Countess of broad lands besides; but this year and more has the Black Knight held her prisoner in her own halls because she would not listen to his suit." "Then lead me to your lady forthwith," cried Sir Owain; "right gladly will I take her quarrel upon me if there be any that will oppose me." So she led him to the Countess' bower, and there he made him known to the fair lady and proffered her his services. And she that had long deemed there was no deliverance for her, accepted them right gladly. So taking her by the hand, he led her down to the hall, and there, standing at the door, he proclaimed her the lawful lady of that castle and all its lands, and himself ready to do battle in her cause. But none answered his challenge, for those that had held with the Black Knight, deprived of their leader, had lost heart, whereas they that for their loyalty to their lady had been held in subjection, gathered fast about Sir Owain, ready to do battle. So in short space, Sir Owain drove forth the lawless invaders of the Countess' lands, and called together her vassals that they might do homage to her anew.

Thus he abode in the castle many days, seeking in all that he might to do her service, until through all her lands order was restored, and her right acknowledged. But when all was done, Sir Owain yet tarried in the lady's castle; for he loved her much, but doubted ever of her favour. So one day, Luned, the damsel who had come to his aid on the day that he slew the Black Knight, said to him: "Alas! Sir Knight, the time must come when ye will leave us. And who will then defend my lady's fountain, which is the key to all her lands? For who holds the fountain, holds the land also." "I will never fail your lady while there is breath in my body," cried Sir Owain. "Then were it well that ye stayed here ever," answered Luned. "Gladly would I," answered Sir Owain, "if that I might." "Ye might find a way if your wits were as sharp as your sword," she answered, and laughing, left him, but herself sought her lady. Long he pondered her words, and he was still deep in thought, when there came to him the Countess, and said: "Sir Knight, I hear that ye must leave us." "Nay, my lady," answered Sir Owain, "I will stay as long as ye require my services." "There must ever be one to guard the fountain, and he who guards the fountain, is lord of these lands," answered the lady softly. Then Sir Owain found words at last, and bending the knee, he said: "Lady, if ye love me, I will stay and guard you and your lands; and if ye love me not, I will go into my own country, and yet will I come again whensoever ye have need of me. For never loved I any but you." Then the Countess bade him stay, and calling her vassals together, she commanded all to do homage to him, and took him for her husband in presence of them all.

Thus Sir Owain won the Lady of the Fountain.

BOOK VII
SIR PEREDUR

CHAPTER XXII
THE ADVENTURES OF SIR PEREDUR

At one time there was in the North of Britain a great Earl named Evrawc. A stout knight he was, and few were the tournaments at which he was not to be found in company with six of his sons; the seventh only, who was too young to bear arms, remaining at home with his mother. But at the last, after he had won the prize at many a tourney, Earl Evrawc was slain, and his six sons with him; and then the Countess fled with Peredur, her youngest, to a lonely spot in the midst of a forest, far from the dwellings of men; for she was minded to bring him up where he might never hear of jousts and feats of arms, that so at least one son might be left to her.

So Peredur was reared amongst women and decrepit old men, and even these were strictly commanded never to tell the boy aught of the great world beyond the forest, or what men did therein. None the less, he grew up active and fearless, as nimble and sure-footed as the goats, and patient of much toil.

Then, one day, when Peredur was grown a tall, strong youth, there chanced what had never chanced before; for there came riding through the forest, hard by where Peredur dwelt with his mother, a knight in full armour, none other, indeed, than the good knight, Sir Owain himself. And seeing him, Peredur cried out: "Mother, what is that, yonder?" "An angel, my son," said his mother. "Then will I go and become an angel with him," said Peredur; and before any one could stay him, he was gone.

When Sir Owain saw him approaching, he reined in his horse, and after courteous salutation, said: "I pray thee, fair youth, tell me, hast thou seen a knight pass this way?" "I know not what a knight may be," answered Peredur. "Why, even such an one as I," answered Sir Owain. "If ye will tell me what I ask you, I will tell you what ye ask me," said Peredur; and when Owain, laughing, consented, Peredur touched the saddle, demanding,

"What is this?" "Surely, a saddle," replied Sir Owain; and, in like manner, Peredur asked him of all the parts of his armour, and Owain answered him patiently and courteously. Then when he had ended his questions, Peredur said: "Ride forward; for yesterday I saw from a distance such an one as ye are, ride through the forest."

Sir Peredur returned to his mother, and exclaimed: "Mother, that was no angel, but a noble knight"; and hearing his words, his mother fell into a swoon. But Peredur hastened to the spot where were tethered the horses that brought them firewood and food from afar, and from them he chose a bony piebald, which seemed the strongest and in the best condition. Then he found a pack and fastened it on the horse's back, in some way to resemble a saddle, and strove with twigs to imitate the trappings he had seen upon Sir Owain's horse. When his preparations were complete, he returned to the Countess, who, by then, was recovered from her swoon; and she saw that all her trouble had been in vain, and that the time was come when she must part with her son. "Thou wilt ride forth, my son?" she asked. "Yea, with your leave," he answered. "Hear, then, my counsel," said she; "go thy way to Arthur's court, for there are the noblest and truest knights. And wheresoever thou seest a church, fail not to say thy prayers, and whatsoever woman demands thy aid, refuse her not."

So, bidding his mother farewell, Peredur mounted his horse, and took in his hand a long, sharp-pointed stake. He journeyed many days till, at last, he had come to Caerleon, where Arthur held his court, and dismounting at the door, he entered the hall. Even as he did so, a stranger knight, who had passed in before him, seized a goblet and, dashing the wine in the face of Queen Guenevere, held the goblet aloft and cried: "If any dare dispute this goblet with me or venture to avenge the insult done to Arthur's Queen, let him follow me to the meadow without, where I will await him."

And for sheer amazement at this insolence, none moved save Peredur, who cried aloud: "I will seek out this man and do vengeance upon him." Then a voice exclaimed: "Welcome, goodly Peredur, thou flower of knighthood"; and all turned in surprise to look upon a little misshapen dwarf, who, a year before, had craved and obtained shelter in Arthur's court, and since then had spoken no word. But Kay the Seneschal, in anger that a mere boy, and one so strangely equipped as Peredur, should have taken up the Queen's quarrel when proven knights had remained mute, struck the dwarf, crying: "Thou art ill-bred to remain mute a year in Arthur's court, and then to break silence in praise of such a fellow." Then Peredur, who saw the blow, cried, as he left the hall: "Knight, hereafter ye shall answer to me for that blow." Therewith, he mounted his piebald and rode in haste to the meadow. And when the knight espied him, he cried to him: "Tell me, youth, saw'st thou any coming after me from the court?" "I am come myself," said Peredur. "Hold thy peace," answered the knight angrily, "and go back to the court and say that, unless one comes in haste, I will not tarry, but will ride away, holding them all shamed." "By my faith," said Peredur, "willingly or unwillingly, thou shalt answer to me for thine insolence; and I will have the goblet of thee, ay, and thy horse and armour to boot." With that, in a rage, the knight struck Peredur a violent blow between the neck and the shoulder with the butt-end of his lance. "So!" cried Peredur, "not thus did my mother's servants play with me; and thus will I play with thee"; and drove at him with his pointed stake that it entered the eye of the knight, who forthwith fell dead from his horse. Then Peredur dismounted and began wrenching at the fastenings of the dead man's armour, for he saw in the adventure the means of equipping himself as a knight should ride; but knowing not the trick of the fastenings, his efforts were in vain. While he yet struggled, there rode up Sir Owain who had followed in hot haste from the court; and when he saw the fallen knight, he was amazed that a mere lad, unarmed and unskilled in knightly exercises, should thus have prevailed. "Fair youth," said he, "what would ye?" "I would have this knight's iron coat, but I cannot stir it for all my efforts." "Nay, young Sir," said Sir Owain, "leave the dead his arms, and take mine and my horse, which I give you right gladly; and come with me to the King to receive the order of knighthood, for, by my faith, ye have shown yourself worthy of it." "I thank you, noble Sir," answered Peredur, "and gladly I accept your gift; but I will not go with you now. Rather will I seek other adventures and prove me further first; nor will I seek the King's presence until I have encountered with the tall knight that so misused the dwarf, and have called him to account. Only, I pray you, take this goblet to Queen Guenevere, and say to my lord, King Arthur, that, in all places and at all times, I am his true vassal, and will render him such service as I may." Then, with Sir Owain's help, Peredur put on the armour, and mounting his horse, after due salutation, rode on his way.

So, for many days, Peredur followed his adventures, and many a knight he met and overthrew. To all he yielded grace, requiring only that they should ride to Caerleon, there to give themselves up to the King's pleasure, and say that Peredur had sent them. At last he came to a fair castle that rose from the shores of a lake, and there he was welcomed by a venerable old man who pressed him to make some stay. So, as they sat at supper, the old man asked Peredur many questions of himself and his adventure, gazing earnestly on him the while; and, at last, he said: "I know thee who thou art. Thou art my sister's son. Stay now with me, and I will teach thee the arts and courtesy and noble bearing of a gentle knight, and give thee the degree when thou art accomplished in all that becomes an honourable knight." Thereto Peredur assented gladly, and remained with his uncle until he had come to a perfect knowledge of chivalry; after that, he received the order of knighthood at the old man's hands, and rode forth again to seek adventures. Presently he came to the city of Caerleon, but though Arthur was there with all his court, Sir Peredur chose to make himself known to none; for he had not yet avenged the dwarf on Sir Kay. Now it chanced, as he walked through the city, he saw at her casement a beautiful maiden whose name was Angharad; and at once he knew that he had seen the damsel whom he must love his life long. So he sought to be acquainted with her, but she scorned him, thinking him but some unproved knight, since he consorted not with those of Arthur's court; and, at last, finding he might in no wise win her favour at that time, he made a vow that never would he speak to Christian man or woman until he had gained her love, and forthwith rode away again. After long journeyings, he came one night to a castle, and, knocking, gained admittance and courteous reception from the lady who owned it. But it seemed to Sir Peredur that there hung over all a gloom, none caring to talk or make merry, though there was no lack of the consideration due to a guest. Then when the evening hour was come, they took their places at the board, Peredur being set at the Countess' right hand; and two nuns entered and placed before the lady a flagon of wine and six white loaves, and that was all the fare. Then the Countess gave largely of the food to Sir Peredur, keeping little for herself and her attendants; but this pleased not the knight, who, heedless of his oath, said: "Lady, permit me to fare as do the others," and he took but a small portion of that which she had given him. Then the Countess, blushing as with shame, said to him: "Sir Knight, if we make you poor cheer, far otherwise is our desire, but we are in sore straits." "Madam," answered Peredur courteously, "for your welcome I thank you heartily; and, I pray you, if there is aught in which a knight may serve you, tell me your trouble." Then the Countess told him how she had been her father's one child, and heir to his broad lands; and how a neighbouring baron had sought her hand; but she, misliking him, had refused his suit, so that his wrath was great. Then, when her father died, he had made war upon her, overrunning all her lands till nothing was left to her but the one castle. Long since, all the provision stored therein was consumed, and she must have yielded her to the oppressor but for the charity of the nuns of a neighbouring monastery, who had secretly supplied her with food when, for fear, her vassals had forsaken her. But that day the nuns had told her that no longer could they aid her, and there was naught left save to submit to the invader. This was the story that, with many tears, the Countess related to Peredur. "Lady," said he, "with your permission, I will take upon me your quarrel, and to-morrow I will seek to encounter this felon." The Countess thanked him heartily and they retired to rest for that night.

In the morning betimes, Sir Peredur arose, donned his armour and, seeking the Countess, desired that the portcullis might be raised, for he would sally forth to seek her oppressor. So he rode out from the castle and saw in the morning light a plain covered with the tents of a great host. With him he took a herald to proclaim that he was ready to meet any in fair fight, in the Countess' quarrel. Forthwith, in answer to his challenge, there rode forward the baron himself, a proud and stately knight mounted on a great black horse. The two rushed together, and, at the first encounter, Sir Peredur unhorsed his opponent, bearing him over the crupper with such force that he lay stunned, as one dead. Then, Peredur, drawing his sword, dismounted and stood over the fallen knight, who, when he was recovered a little, asked his mercy. "Gladly will I grant it," answered Peredur, "but on these conditions. Ye shall disband this host, restore to the Countess threefold all of which ye have deprived her, and, finally, ye shall submit yourself unto her as her vassal." All this the baron promised to do, and Peredur remained with the Countess in her castle until she was firmly established in that which was rightfully hers. Then he bade her farewell, promising his aid if ever she should need his services, and so rode forth again.

And as he rode, at times he was troubled, thinking on the scorn with which the fair Angharad had treated him, and reproaching himself bitterly for having broken his vow of silence. So he journeyed many days, and at length, one morn, dismounting by a little woodland stream, he stood lost in thought, heedless of his surroundings. Now, as it chanced, Arthur and a company of his knights were encamped hard by; for, returning from an expedition, the King had been told of Peredur and how he had taken upon him the Queen's quarrel, and forthwith had ridden out in search of him. When the King espied Sir Peredur standing near the brook, he said to the knights about him: "Know ye yonder knight?" "I know him not," said Sir Kay, "but I will soon learn his name." So he rode up to Sir Peredur and spoke to him, demanding his name. When Peredur answered not, though questioned more than once, Sir Kay in anger, struck him with the butt-end of his spear. On the instant, Sir Peredur caught him with his lance under the jaw, and, though himself unmounted, hurled Kay from the saddle. Then when Kay returned not, Sir Owain mounted his horse and rode forth to learn what had happened, and by the brook he found Sir Kay sore hurt, and Peredur ready mounted to encounter any who sought a quarrel. But at once Sir Owain recognised Sir Peredur and rejoiced to see him; and when he found Sir Peredur would speak no word, being himself an honourable knight, he thought no evil, but urged him to ride back with him to Arthur's camp. And Sir Peredur, still speaking never a word, went with Sir Owain, and all respected his silence save Kay, who was long healing of the injuries he had received, and whose angry words none heeded. So they returned to Caerleon and soon, through the city, were noised the noble deeds of Sir Peredur, each new-comer bringing some fresh story of his prowess. Then when Angharad learnt how true and famous was the knight whom she had lightly esteemed, she was sore ashamed; and seeing him ever foremost in the tournament and courteous to all in deed, though speaking not a word; she thought that never had there been so noble a knight, or one so worthy of a lady's love. Thus in the winning of her favour, Sir Peredur was released from his vow, and his marriage was celebrated with much pomp before the King and Queen. Long and happily he lived, famed through all Britain as one of the most valiant and faithful knights of King Arthur's Round Table.

BOOK VIII
THE HOLY GRALL

CHAPTER XXIII
THE COMING OF SIR GALAHAD

Many times had the Feast of Pentecost come round, and many were the knights that Arthur had made since first he founded the Order of the Round Table; yet no knight had appeared who dared claim the seat named by Merlin the Siege Perilous. At last, one vigil of the great feast, a lady came to Arthur's court at Camelot and asked Sir Launcelot to ride with her into the forest hard by, for a purpose not then to be revealed. Launcelot consenting, they rode together until they came to a nunnery hidden deep in the forest; and there the lady bade Launcelot dismount, and led him into a great and stately room. Presently there entered twelve nuns and with them a youth, the fairest that Launcelot had ever seen. "Sir," said the nuns, "we have brought up this child in our midst, and now that he is grown to manhood, we pray you make him knight, for of none worthier could he receive the honour." "Is this thy own desire?" asked Launcelot of the young squire; and when he said that so it was, Launcelot promised to make him knight after the great festival had been celebrated in the church next day.

So on the morrow, after they had worshipped, Launcelot knighted Galahad—for that was the youth's name—and asked him if he would ride at once with him to the King's court; but the young knight excusing himself, Sir Launcelot rode back alone to Camelot, where all rejoiced that he was returned in time to keep the feast with the whole Order of the Round Table.

Now, according to his custom, King Arthur was waiting for some marvel to befall before he and his knights sat down to the banquet. Presently a squire entered the hall and said: "Sir King, a great wonder has appeared. There floats on the river a mighty stone, as it were a block of red marble, and it is thrust through by a sword, the hilt of which is set thick with precious stones." On hearing this, the King and all his knights went forth to view the stone and found it as the squire had said; moreover, looking closer, they read these words: "None shall draw me hence, but only he by whose side I must hang; and he shall be the best knight in all the world." Immediately, all bade Launcelot draw forth the sword, but he refused, saying that the sword was not for him. Then, at the King's command, Sir Gawain made the attempt and failed, as did Sir Percivale after him. So the knights knew the adventure was not for them, and returning to the hall, took their places about the Round Table.

No sooner were they seated than an aged man, clothed all in white, entered the hall, followed by a young knight in red armour, by whose side hung an empty scabbard. The old man approached King Arthur and bowing low before him, said: "Sir, I bring you a young knight of the house and lineage of Joseph of Arimathea, and through him shall great glory be won for all the land of Britain." Greatly did King Arthur rejoice to hear this, and welcomed the two right royally. Then when the young knight had saluted the King, the old man led him to the Siege Perilous and drew off its silken cover; and all the knights were amazed, for they saw that where had been engraved the words, "The Siege Perilous," was written now in shining gold: "This is the Siege of the noble prince, Sir Galahad." Straightway the young man seated himself there where none other had ever sat without danger to his life; and all who saw it said, one to another: "Surely this is he that shall achieve the Holy Grail." Now the Holy Grail was the blessed dish from which Our Lord had eaten the Last Supper, and it had been brought to the land of Britain by Joseph of Arimathea; but because of men's sinfulness, it had been withdrawn from human sight, only that, from time to time, it appeared to the pure in heart.

When all had partaken of the royal banquet, King Arthur bade Sir Galahad come with him to the river's brink; and showing him the floating stone with the sword thrust through it, told him how his knights had failed to draw forth the sword. "Sir," said Galahad, "it is no marvel that they failed, for the adventure was meant for me, as my empty scabbard shows." So saying, lightly he drew the sword from the heart of the stone, and lightly he slid it into the scabbard at his side. While all yet wondered at this adventure of the sword, there came riding to them a lady on a white palfrey who, saluting King Arthur, said: "Sir King, Nacien the hermit sends thee word that this day shall great honour be shown to thee and all thine house; for the Holy Grail shall appear in thy hall, and thou and all thy fellowship shall be fed therefrom." And to Launcelot she said: "Sir Knight, thou hast ever been the best knight of all the world; but another has come to whom thou must yield precedence." Then Launcelot answered humbly: "I know well I was never the best." "Ay, of a truth thou wast and art still, of sinful men," said she, and rode away before any could question her further.

So, that evening, when all were gathered about the Round Table, each knight in his own siege, suddenly there was heard a crash of thunder, so mighty that the hall trembled, and there flashed into the hall a sun-beam, brighter far than any that had ever before been seen; and then, draped all in white samite, there glided through the air what none might see, yet what all knew to be the Holy Grail. And all the air was filled with sweet odours, and on every one was shed a light in which he looked fairer and nobler than ever before. So they sat in an amazed silence, till presently King Arthur rose and gave thanks to God for the grace given to him and to his court. Then up sprang Sir Gawain and made his avow to follow for a year and a day the Quest of the Holy Grail, if perchance he might be granted the vision of it. Immediately other of the knights followed his example, binding themselves to the Quest of the Holy Grail until, in all, one hundred and fifty had vowed themselves to the adventure.

Then was King Arthur grieved, for he foresaw the ruin of his noble Order. And turning to Sir Gawain, he said: "Nephew ye have done ill, for through you I am bereft of the noblest company of knights that ever brought honour to any realm in Christendom. Well I know that never again shall all of you gather in this hall, and it grieves me to lose men I have loved as my life and through whom I have won peace and righteousness for all my realm." So the King mourned and his knights with him, but their oaths they could not recall.

CHAPTER XXIV
HOW SIR GALAHAD WON THE RED CROSS SHIELD

Great woe was there in Camelot next day when, after worship in the Cathedral, the knights who had vowed themselves to the Quest of the Holy Grail got to horse and rode away. A goodly company it was that passed through the streets, the townfolk weeping to see them go; Sir Launcelot du Lac and his kin, Sir Galahad of whom all expected great deeds, Sir Bors and Sir Percivale, and many another scarcely less famed than they. So they rode together that day to the Castle of Vagon, where they were entertained right hospitably, and the next day they separated, each to ride his own way and see what adventures should befall him.

So it came to pass that, after four days' ride, Sir Galahad reached an abbey. Now Sir Galahad was still clothed in red armour as when he came to the King's court, and by his side hung the wondrous sword; but he was without a shield. They of the abbey received him right heartily, as also did the brave King Bagdemagus, Knight of the Round Table, who was resting there. When they had greeted each other, Sir Galahad asked King Bagdemagus what adventure had brought him there. "Sir," said Bagdemagus, "I was told that in this abbey was preserved a wondrous shield which none but the best knight in the world might bear without grievous harm to himself. And though I know well that there are better knights than I, to-morrow I purpose to make the attempt. But, I pray you, bide at this monastery awhile until you hear from me; and if I fail, do ye take the adventure upon you." "So be it," said Sir Galahad.

The next day, at their request, Sir Galahad and King Bagdemagus were led into the church by a monk and shown where, behind the altar, hung the wondrous shield, whiter than snow save for the blood-red cross in its midst. Then the monk warned them of the danger to any who, being unworthy, should dare to bear the shield. But King Bagdemagus made answer: "I know well that I am not the best knight in the world, yet will I try if I may bear it." So he hung it about his neck, and, bidding farewell, rode away with his squire.

The two had not journeyed far before they saw a knight approach, armed all in white mail and mounted upon a white horse. Immediately he laid his spear in rest and, charging King Bagdemagus, pierced him through the shoulder and bore him from his horse; and standing over the wounded knight, he said: "Knight, thou hast shown great folly, for none shall bear this shield save the peerless knight, Sir Galahad." Then, taking the shield, he gave it to the squire and said: "Bear this shield to the good Knight Galahad and greet him well from me." "What is your name?" asked the squire, "That is not for thee or any other to know." "One thing, I pray you," said the squire; "why may this shield be borne by none but Sir Galahad without danger?" "Because it belongs to him only," answered the stranger knight, and vanished.

Then the squire took the shield and, setting King Bagdemagus on his horse, bore him back to the abbey where he lay long, sick unto death. To Galahad the squire gave the shield and told him all that had befallen. So Galahad hung the shield about his neck and rode the way that Bagdemagus had gone the day before; and presently he met the White Knight, whom he greeted courteously, begging that he would make known to him the marvels of the red-cross shield. "That will I gladly," answered the White Knight. "Ye must know, Sir Knight, that this shield was made and given by Joseph of Arimathea to the good King Evelake of Sarras, that, in the might of the holy symbol, he should overthrow the heathen who threatened his kingdom. But afterwards, King Evelake followed Joseph to this land of Britain where they taught the true faith unto the people who before were heathen. Then when Joseph lay dying, he bade King Evelake set the shield in the monastery where ye lay last night, and foretold that none should wear it without loss until that day when it should be taken by the knight, ninth and last in descent from him, who should come to that place the fifteenth day after receiving the degree of knighthood. Even so has it been with you, Sir Knight." So saying, the unknown knight disappeared and Sir Galahad rode on his way.

CHAPTER XXV
THE ADVENTURES OF SIR PERCIVALE

After he had left his fellows, Sir Percivale rode long through the forest until, one evening, he reached a monastery where he sought shelter for the night. The next morning, he went into the chapel to hear mass and there he espied the body of an old, old man, laid on a richly adorned couch. At first it seemed as if the aged man were dead, but presently, raising himself in his bed, he took off his crown, and, delivering it to the priest, bade him place it on the altar. So when the service was concluded, Sir Percivale asked who the aged king might be. Then he was told that it was none other than King Evelake who accompanied Joseph of Arimathea to Britain. And on a certain occasion, the King had approached the Holy Grail nigher than was reverent and, for his impiety, God had punished him with blindness. Thereupon he repented and, entreating God earnestly, had obtained his petition that he should not die until he had seen the spotless knight who should be descended from him in the ninth degree. (This his desire was fulfilled later when Sir Galahad came thither; after which, he died and was buried by the good knight.)

The next day, Sir Percivale continued his journey and presently met with twenty knights who bore on a bier the body of a dead knight. When they espied Sir Percivale, they demanded of him who he was and whence he came. So he told them, whereupon they all shouted, "Slay him! slay him!" and setting upon him all at once, they killed his horse and would have slain him but that the good knight, Sir Galahad, passing that way by chance, came to his rescue and put his assailants to flight. Then Galahad rode away as fast as he might, for he would not be thanked, and Sir Percivale was left, horseless and alone, in the forest.

So Sir Percivale continued his journey on foot as well as he might; and ever the way became lonelier, until at last he came to the shores of a vast sea. There Sir Percivale abode many days, without food and desolate, doubting whether he should ever escape thence. At last it chanced that, looking out to sea, Sir Percivale descried a ship and, as it drew nearer, he saw how it was all hung with satin and velvet. Presently, it reached the land and out of it there stepped a lady of marvellous beauty, who asked him how he came there; "For know," said she, "ye are like to die here by hunger or mischance." "He whom I serve will protect me," said Sir Percivale. "I know well whom ye desire most to see," said the lady. "Ye would meet with the Red Knight who bears the red-cross shield." "Ah! lady, I pray you tell me where I may find him," cried Sir Percivale. "With a good will," said the damsel; "if ye will but promise me your service when I shall ask for it, I will lead you to the knight, for I met him of late in the forest." So Sir Percivale promised gladly to serve her when she should need him. Then the lady asked him how long he had fasted. "For three days," answered Sir Percivale. Immediately she gave orders to her attendants forthwith to pitch a tent and set out a table with all manner of delicacies, and of these she invited Sir Percivale to partake. "I pray you, fair lady," said Sir Percivale, "who are ye that show me such kindness?" "Truly," said the lady, "I am but a hapless damsel, driven forth from my inheritance by a great lord whom I have chanced to displease. I implore you, Sir Knight, by your vows of knighthood, to give me your aid." Sir Percivale promised her all the aid he could give, and then she bade him lie down and sleep, and herself took off his helmet, and unclasped his sword-belt. So Sir Percivale slept, and when he waked, there was another feast prepared, and he was given the rarest and the strongest wines that ever he had tasted. Thus they made merry and, when the lady begged Percivale to rest him there awhile, promising him all that ever he could desire if he would vow himself to her service, almost he forgot the quest to which he was vowed, and would have consented, but that his eye fell upon his sword where it lay. Now in the sword-hilt there was set a red cross and, seeing it, Percivale called to mind his vow, and, thinking on it, he signed him with the cross on his forehead. Instantly, the tent was overthrown and vanished in thick smoke; and she who had appeared a lovely woman disappeared from his sight in semblance of a fiend.

Then was Sir Percivale sore ashamed that almost he had yielded to the temptings of the Evil One, and earnestly, he prayed that his sin might be forgiven him. Thus he remained in prayer far into the night, bewailing his weakness; and when the dawn appeared, a ship drew nigh the land. Sir Percivale entered into it, but could find no one there; so commending himself to God, he determined to remain thereon, and was borne over the seas for many days, he knew not whither.

CHAPTER XXVI
THE ADVENTURES OF SIR BORS

Among the knights vowed to the Quest of the Holy Grail was Sir Bors, one of the kin of Sir Launcelot, a brave knight and pious. He rode through the forest many a day, making his lodging most often under a leafy tree, though once on his journey he stayed at a castle, that he might do battle for its lady against a felon knight who would have robbed and oppressed her.

So, on a day, as he rode through the forest, Sir Bors came to the parting of two ways. While he was considering which he should follow, he espied two knights driving before them a horse on which was stretched, bound and naked, none other than Sir Bors' own brother, Sir Lionel; and, from time to time, the two false knights beat him with thorns so that his body was all smeared with blood, but, so great was his heart, Sir Lionel uttered never a word. Then, in great wrath, Sir Bors laid his lance in rest and would have fought the felon knights to rescue his brother, but that, even as he spurred his horse, there came a bitter cry from the other path and, looking round, he saw a lady being dragged by a knight into the darkest part of the forest where none might find and rescue her. When she saw Sir Bors, she cried to him: "Help me! Sir Knight, help me! I beseech you by your knighthood." Then Sir Bors was much troubled, for he would not desert his brother; but bethinking him that ever a woman must be more helpless than a man, he wheeled his horse, rode upon her captor and beat him to the earth. The damsel thanked him earnestly and told him how the knight was her own cousin, who had that day carried her off by craft from her father's castle. As they talked, there came up twelve knights who had been seeking the lady everywhere; so to their care Sir Bors delivered her, and rode with haste in the direction whither his brother had been borne. On the way, he met with an old man, dressed as a priest, who asked him what he sought. When Sir Bors had told him, "Ah! Bors," said he, "I can give you tidings indeed. Your brother is dead"; and parting the bushes, he showed him the body of a dead man, to all seeming Sir Lionel's self. Then Sir Bors grieved sorely, misdoubting almost whether he should not have rescued his own brother rather than the lady; and at the last, he dug a grave and buried the dead man; after which he rode sorrowfully on his way.

When he had ridden many days, he met with a yeoman whom he asked if there were any adventures in those parts. "Sir," said the man, "at the castle; hard by, they hold a great tournament." Sir Bors thanked him and rode along the way pointed out to him; and presently, as he passed a hermitage, whom should he see sitting at its door but his brother, Sir Lionel, whom he had believed dead. Then in great joy, he leaped from his horse, and running to Lionel, cried: "Fair brother, how came ye hither?" "Through no aid of yours," said Sir Lionel angrily; "for ye left me bound and beaten, to ride to the rescue of a maiden. Never was brother so dealt with by brother before. Keep you from me as ye may!" When Sir Bors understood that his brother would slay him, he knelt before him entreating his pardon. Sir Lionel took no heed, but mounting his horse and taking his lance, cried: "Keep you from me, traitor! Fight, or die!" And Sir Bors moved not; for to him it seemed a sin most horrible that brother should fight with brother. Then Sir Lionel, in his rage, rode his horse at him, bore him to the ground and trampled him under the horse's hoofs, till Bors lay beaten to the earth in a swoon. Even so, Sir Lionel's anger was not stayed; for, alighting, he drew his sword and would have smitten off his brother's head, but that the holy hermit, hearing the noise of conflict, ran out of the hermitage and threw himself upon Sir Bors. "Gentle knight," he cried, "have mercy upon him and on thyself; for of the sin of slaying thy brother, thou couldst never be quit." "Sir Priest," said Lionel, "if ye leave him not, I shall slay you too." "It were a lesser sin than to slay thy brother," answered the hermit. "So be it," cried Lionel, and with one blow, struck off the hermit's head. Then he would have worked his evil will upon his brother too, but that, even as he was unlacing Sir Bors' helm to cut off his head, there rode up the good knight Sir Colgrevance, a fellow of the Round Table. When he saw the dead hermit and was aware how Lionel sought the life of Bors, he was amazed, and springing from his horse, ran to Lionel and dragged him back from his brother. "Do ye think to hinder me?" said Sir Lionel. "Let come who will, I will have his life." "Ye shall have to do with me first," cried Colgrevance. Therewith, they took their swords, and, setting their shields before them, rushed upon each other. Now Sir Colgrevance was a good knight, but Sir Lionel was strong and his anger added to his strength. So long they fought that Sir Bors had time to recover from his swoon, and raising himself with pain on his elbow, saw how the two fought for his life; and as it seemed, Sir Lionel would prevail, for Sir Colgrevance grew weak and weary. Sir Bors tried to get to his feet, but, so weak he was, he could not stand; and Sir Colgrevance, seeing him stir, called on him to come to his aid, for he was in mortal peril for his sake. But even as he called, Sir Lionel cut him to the ground and, as one possessed, rushed upon his brother to slay him. Sir Bors entreated him for mercy, and when he would not, sorrowfully he took his sword, saying: "Now, God forgive me, though I defend my life against my brother."

Immediately there was heard a voice saying, "Flee, Bors, and touch not thy brother"; and at the same time, a fiery cloud burned between them, so that their shields glowed with the flame, and both knights fell to the earth. But the voice came again, saying, "Bors, leave thy brother and take thy way to the sea. There thou shalt meet Sir Percivale." Then Sir Bors made ready to obey, and, turning to Lionel, said: "Dear brother, I pray you forgive me for aught in which I have wronged you." "I forgive you," said Lionel, for he was too amazed and terrified to keep his anger.

So Sir Bors continued his journey, and at the last, coming to the sea shore, he espied a ship, draped all with white samite, and entering thereon, he saw Sir Percivale, and much they rejoiced them in each other's company.

CHAPTER XXVII
THE ADVENTURES OF SIR LAUNCELOT

After Sir Launcelot had parted from his fellows at the Castle of Vagon, he rode many days through the forest without adventure, till he chanced upon a knight close by a little hermitage in the wood. Immediately, as was the wont of errant knights, they prepared to joust, and Launcelot, whom none before had overthrown, was borne down, man and horse, by the stranger knight. Thereupon a nun, who dwelt in the hermitage, cried: "God be with thee, best knight in all this world," for she knew the victor for Sir Galahad. But Galahad, not wishing to be known, rode swiftly away; and presently Sir Launcelot got to horse again and rode slowly on his way, shamed and doubting sorely in his heart whether this quest were meant for him.

When night fell, he came to a great stone cross which stood at the parting of the way and close by a little ruined chapel. So Sir Launcelot, being minded to pass the night there, alighted, fastened his horse to a tree and hung his shield on a bough. Then he drew near to the little chapel, and wondered to see how, all ruinous though it was, yet within was an altar hung with silk and a great silver candlestick on it; but when he sought entrance, he could find none and, much troubled in his mind, he returned to his horse where he had left it, and unlacing his helm and ungirding his sword, laid him down to rest.

Then it seemed to Sir Launcelot that, as he lay between sleeping and waking, there passed him two white palfreys bearing a litter wherein was a sick knight, who cried: "Sweet Lord, when shall I be pardoned all my transgressions, and when shall the holy vessel come to me, to cure me of my sickness?" And instantly it seemed that the great candlestick came forth of itself from the chapel, floating through the air before a table of silver on which was the Holy Grail. Thereupon the sick knight raised himself, and on his bended knees he approached so nigh that he kissed the holy vessel; and immediately he cried: "I thank Thee, sweet Lord, that I am healed of my sickness." And all the while Sir Launcelot, who saw this wonder, felt himself held that he could not move. Then a squire brought the stranger knight his weapons, in much joy that his lord was cured. "Who think ye that this knight may be who remains sleeping when the holy vessel is so near?" said the knight. "In truth," said the squire, "he must be one that is held by the bond of some great sin. I will take his helm and his sword, for here have I brought you all your armour save only these two." So the knight armed him from head to foot, and taking Sir Launcelot's horse, rode away with his squire. On the instant, Sir Launcelot awoke amazed, not knowing whether he had dreamed or not; but while he wondered, there came a terrible voice, saying: "Launcelot, arise and leave this holy place." In shame, Sir Launcelot turned to obey, only to find horse and sword and shield alike vanished. Then, indeed, he knew himself dishonoured. Weeping bitterly, he made the best of his way on foot, until he came to a cell where a hermit was saying prayer. Sir Launcelot knelt too, and, when all was ended, called to the hermit, entreating him for counsel. "With good will," said the hermit. So Sir Launcelot made himself known and told the hermit all, lamenting how his good fortune was turned to wretchedness and his glory to shame; and truly, the hermit was amazed that Sir Launcelot should be in such case. "Sir," said he, "God has given you manhood and strength beyond all other knights; the more are ye bounden to his service." "I have sinned," said Sir Launcelot; "for in all these years of my knighthood, I have done everything for the honour and glory of my lady and naught for my Maker; and little thank have I given to God for all his benefits to me." Then the holy man gave Sir Launcelot good counsel and made him rest there that night; and the next day he gave him a horse, a sword and a helmet, and bade him go forth and bear himself knightly as the servant of God.

CHAPTER XXVIII
HOW SIR LAUNCELOT SAW THE HOLY GRAIL

For many days after he had left the hermitage, Sir Launcelot rode through the forest, but there came to him no such adventures as had befallen him on other quests to the increase of his fame. At last, one night-tide, he came to the shores of a great water and there he lay down to sleep; but as he slept, a voice called on him: "Launcelot, arise, put on thine armour and go on thy way until thou comest to a ship. Into that thou shalt enter." Immediately, Sir Launcelot started from his sleep to obey and, riding along the shore, came presently to a ship beached on the strand; no sooner had he entered it, than the ship was launched—how, he might not know. So the ship sailed before the wind for many a day. No mortal was on it, save only Sir Launcelot, yet were all his needs supplied. Then, at last, the ship ran ashore at the foot of a great castle; and it was midnight. Sir Launcelot waited not for the dawn, but, his sword gripped in his hand, sprang ashore, and then, right before him, he saw a postern where the gate stood open indeed, but two grisly lions kept the way. And when Sir Launcelot would have rushed upon the great beasts with his sword, it was struck from his hand, and a voice said: "Ah! Launcelot, ever is thy trust in thy might rather than thy Maker!" Sore ashamed, Sir Launcelot took his sword and thrust it back into the sheath, and going forward, he passed unhurt through the gateway, the lions that kept it falling back from his path. So without more adventure, Launcelot entered into the castle; and there he saw how every door stood open, save only one, and that was fast barred, nor, with all his force, might he open it. Presently from the chamber within came the sound of a sweet voice in a holy chant, and then in his heart Launcelot knew that he was come to the Holy Grail. So, kneeling humbly, he prayed that to him might be shown some vision of that he sought. Forthwith the door flew open and from the chamber blazed a light such as he had never known before; but when he made to enter, a voice cried: "Launcelot, forbear," and sorrowfully he withdrew. Then where he knelt, far even from the threshold of the wondrous room, he saw a silver table and, on it, covered with red samite, the Holy Grail. At sight of that which he had sought so long, his joy became so great that, unmindful of the warning, he advanced into the room and drew nigh even to the Table itself. Then on the instant there burst between him and it a blaze of light, and he fell to the ground. There he lay, nor might he move nor utter any sound; only he was aware of hands busy about him which bore him away from the chamber.

For four-and-twenty days, Sir Launcelot lay as in a trance. At the end of that time, he came to himself, and found those about him that had tended him in his swoon. These, when they had given him fresh raiment, brought him to the aged King—Pelles was his name—that owned that castle. The King entertained him right royally, for he knew of the fame of Sir Launcelot; and long he talked with him of his quest and of the other knights who followed it, for he was of a great age and knew much of men. At the end of four days, he spoke to Sir Launcelot, bidding him return to Arthur's court; "For," said he, "your quest is ended here, and all that ye shall see of the Holy Grail, ye have seen." So Launcelot rode on his way, grieving for the sin that hindered him from the perfect vision of the Holy Grail, but thanking God for that which he had seen. So in time he came to Camelot, and told to Arthur all that had befallen him.

CHAPTER XXIX
THE END OF THE QUEST

After he had rescued Sir Percivale from the twenty knights who beset him, Sir Galahad rode on his way till night-fall, when he sought shelter at a little hermitage. Thither there came in the night a damsel who desired to speak with Sir Galahad; so he arose and went to her, "Galahad," said she, "arm you and mount your horse and follow me, for I am come to guide you in your quest." So they rode together until they had come to the sea-shore, and there the damsel showed Galahad a great ship into which he must enter. Then she bade him farewell, and he, going on to the ship, found there already the good knights Sir Bors and Sir Percivale, who made much joy of the meeting. They abode in that ship until they had come to the castle of King Pelles, who welcomed them right gladly. Then, as they all sat at supper that night, suddenly the hall was filled with a great light, and the holy vessel appeared in their midst, covered all in white samite. While they all rejoiced, there came a voice saying: "My Knights whom I have chosen, ye have seen the holy vessel dimly. Continue your journey to the city of Sarras and there the perfect Vision shall be yours."

Now in the city of Sarras had dwelt long time Joseph of Arimathea, teaching its people the true faith, before ever he came into the land of Britain; but when Sir Galahad and his fellows came there after long voyage, they found it ruled by a heathen king named Estorause, who cast them into a deep dungeon. There they were kept a year, but at the end of that time, the tyrant died. Then the great men of the land gathered together to consider who should be their king; and, while they were in council, came a voice bidding them take as their king the youngest of the three knights whom Estorause had thrown into prison. So in fear and wonder they hastened to the prison, and releasing the three knights, made Galahad king as the voice had bidden them.

Thus Sir Galahad became King of the famous city of Sarras, in far Babylon. He had reigned a year when, one morning early, he and the other two knights, his fellows, went into the chapel, and there they saw, kneeling in prayer, an aged man, robed as a bishop, and round him hovered many angels. The knights fell on their knees in awe and reverence, whereupon he that seemed a bishop turned to them and said: "I am Joseph of Arimathea, and I am come to show you the perfect Vision of the Holy Grail." On the instant there appeared before them, without veil or cover, the holy vessel, in a radiance of light such as almost blinded them. Sir Bors and Sir Percivale, when at length they were recovered from the brightness of that glory, looked up to find that the holy Joseph and the wondrous vessel had passed from their sight. Then they went to Sir Galahad where he still knelt as in prayer, and behold, he was dead; for it had been with him even as he had prayed; in the moment when he had seen the vision, his soul had gone back to God.

So the two knights buried him in that far city, themselves mourning and all the people with them. And immediately after, Sir Percivale put off his arms and took the habit of a monk, living a devout and holy life until, a year and two months later, he also died and was buried near Sir Galahad. Then Sir Bors armed him, and bidding farewell to the city, sailed away until, after many weeks, he came again to the land of Britain. There he took horse, and stayed not till he had come to Camelot. Great was the rejoicing of Arthur and all his knights when Sir Bors was once more among them. When he had told all the adventures which had befallen him and the good knights, his companions, all who heard were filled with amaze. But the King, he caused the wisest clerks in the land to write in great hooks this Quest of the Holy Grail, that the fame of it should endure unto all time.

BOOK IX
THE FAIR MAID OF ASTOLAT

CHAPTER XXX
THE FAIR MAID OF ASTOLAT

At last, the Quest of the Holy Grail was ended, and by ones and twos the knights came back to Camelot, though many who had set out so boldly were never seen again about the Round Table.

Great was the joy of King Arthur when Sir Launcelot and Sir Bors returned, for, so long had they been away, that almost he had feared that they had perished. In their honour there was high festival for many days in London, where Arthur then had his court; and the King made proclamation of a great tournament that he would hold at Camelot, when he and the King of Northgalis would keep the lists against all comers.

So, one fair morning of spring, King Arthur made ready to ride to Camelot and all his knights with him, save Launcelot, who excused himself, saying that an old wound hindered him from riding. But when the King, sore vexed, had departed, the Queen rebuked Sir Launcelot, and bade him go and prove his great prowess as of old. "Madam," said Sir Launcelot, "in this, as in all else, I obey you; at your bidding I go, but know that in this tournament I shall adventure me in other wise than ever before."

The next day, at dawn, Sir Launcelot mounted his horse, and, riding forth unattended, journeyed all that day till, as evening fell, he reached the little town of Astolat, and there, at the castle, sought lodgement for that night. The old Lord of Astolat was glad at his coming, judging him at once to be a noble knight, though he knew him not, for it was Sir Launcelot's will to remain unknown.

So they went to supper, Sir Launcelot and the old lord, his son, Sir Lavaine, and his daughter Elaine, whom they of the place called the Fair Maid of Astolat. As they sat at meat, the Baron asked Sir Launcelot if he rode to the tournament. "Yea," answered Launcelot; "and right glad should I be if, of your courtesy, ye would lend me a shield without device." "Right willingly," said his host; "ye shall have my son, Sir Tirre's shield. He was but lately made knight and was hurt in his first encounter, so his shield is bare enough. If ye will take with you my young son, Sir Lavaine, he will be glad to ride in the company of so noble a knight and will do you such service as he may." "I shall be glad indeed of his fellowship," answered Sir Launcelot courteously.

Now it seemed to the fair Elaine that never had she beheld so noble a knight as this stranger; and seeing that he was as gentle and courteous as he was strong, she said to him: "Fair Knight, will ye wear my favour at this tournament? For never have I found knight yet to wear my crimson sleeve, and sure am I that none other could ever win it such honour." "Maiden," said Sir Launcelot, "right gladly would I serve you in aught; but it has never been my custom to wear lady's favour." "Then shall it serve the better for disguise," answered Elaine. Sir Launcelot pondered her words, and at last he said: "Fair maiden, I will do for you what I have done for none, and will wear your favour." So with great glee, she brought it him, a crimson velvet sleeve embroidered with great pearls, and fastened it in his helmet. Then Sir Launcelot begged her to keep for him his own shield until after the tournament, when he would come for it again and tell them his name.

The next morn, Sir Launcelot took his departure with Sir Lavaine and, by evening, they were come to Camelot. Forthwith Sir Lavaine led Sir Launcelot to the house of a worthy burgher, where he might stay in privacy, undiscovered by those of his acquaintance. Then, when at dawn the trumpets blew, they mounted their horses and rode to a little wood hard by the lists, and there they abode some while; for Sir Launcelot would take no part until he had seen which side was the stronger. So they saw how King Arthur sat high on a throne to overlook the combat, while the King of Northgalis and all the fellowship of the Round Table held the lists against their opponents led by King Anguish of Ireland and the King of Scots.

Then it soon appeared that the two Kings with all their company could do but little against the Knights of the Round Table, and were sore pressed to maintain their ground. Seeing this, Sir Launcelot said to Sir Lavaine: "Sir Knight, will ye give me your aid if I go to the rescue of the weaker side? For it seems to me they may not much longer hold their own unaided." "Sir," answered Lavaine, "I will gladly follow you and do what I may." So the two laid their lances in rest and charged into the thickest of the fight and, with one spear, Sir Launcelot bore four knights from the saddle. Lavaine, too, did nobly, for he unhorsed the bold Sir Bedivere and Sir Lucan the Butler. Then with their swords they smote lustily on the left hand and on the right, and those whom they had come to aid rallying to them, they drove the Knights of the Round Table back a space. So the fight raged furiously,

Launcelot ever being in the thickest of the press and performing such deeds of valour that all marvelled to see him, and would fain know who was the Knight of the Crimson Sleeve. But the knights of Arthur's court felt shame of their discomfiture, and, in especial, those of Launcelot's kin were wroth that one should appear who seemed mightier even than Launcelot's self. So they called to each other and, making a rally, directed all their force against the stranger knight who had so turned the fortunes of the day. With lances in rest, Sir Lionel, Sir Bors, and Sir Ector, bore down together upon Sir Launcelot, and Sir Bors' spear pierced Sir Launcelot and brought him to the earth, leaving the spear head broken off in his side. This Sir Lavaine saw, and immediately, with all his might, he rode upon the King of Scots, unhorsed him and took his horse to Sir Launcelot. Now Sir Launcelot felt as if he had got his death-wound, but such was his spirit that he was resolved to do some great deed while yet his strength remained. So, with Lavaine's aid, he got upon the horse, took a spear and, laying it in rest, bore down, one after the other, Sir Bors, Sir Lionel, and Sir Ector. Next he flung him into the thickest of the fight, and before the trumpets sounded the signal to cease, he had unhorsed thirty good knights.

Then the Kings of Scotland and Ireland came to Sir Launcelot and said: "Sir Knight, we thank you for the service done us this day. And now, we pray you, come with us to receive the prize which is rightly yours; for never have we seen such deeds as ye have done this day." "My fair lords," answered Sir Launcelot, "for aught that I have accomplished, I am like to pay dearly; I beseech you, suffer me to depart." With these words, he rode away full gallop, followed by Sir Lavaine; and when he had come to a little wood, he called Lavaine to him, saying: "Gentle Knight, I entreat you, draw forth this spear head, for it nigh slayeth me." "Oh! my dear lord," said Lavaine, "I fear sore to draw it forth lest ye die." "If ye love me, draw it out," answered Launcelot. So Lavaine did as he was bidden, and, with a deathly groan, Sir Launcelot fell in a swoon to the ground. When he was a little recovered, he begged Lavaine to help him to his horse and lead him to a hermitage hard by where dwelt a hermit who, in bygone days, had been known to Launcelot for a good knight and true. So with pain and difficulty they journeyed to the hermitage, Lavaine oft fearing that Sir Launcelot would die. And when the hermit saw Sir Launcelot, all pale and besmeared with blood, he scarce knew him for the bold Sir Launcelot du Lac; but he bore him within and dressed his wound and bade him be of good cheer, for he should recover. So there Sir Launcelot abode many weeks and Sir Lavaine with him; for Lavaine would not leave him, such love had he for the good knight he had taken for his lord.

Now when it was known that the victorious knight had departed from the field sore wounded, Sir Gawain vowed to go in search of him. So it chanced that, in his wanderings, he came to Astolat, and there he had a hearty welcome of the Lord of Astolat, who asked him for news of the tournament. Then Sir Gawain related how two stranger knights, bearing white shields, had won great glory, and in especial one, who wore in his helm a crimson sleeve, had surpassed all others in knightly prowess. At these words, the fair Elaine cried aloud with delight. "Maiden," said Gawain, "know ye this knight?" "Not his name," she replied; "but full sure was I that he was a noble knight when I prayed him to wear my favour." Then she showed Gawain the shield which she had kept wrapped in rich broideries, and immediately Sir Gawain knew it for Launcelot's. "Alas!" cried he, "without doubt it was Launcelot himself that we wounded to the death. Sir Bors will never recover the woe of it."

Then, on the morrow, Sir Gawain rode to London to tell the court how the stranger knight and Launcelot were one; but the Fair Maid of Astolat rose betimes, and having obtained leave of her father, set out to search for Sir Launcelot and her brother Lavaine. After many journeyings, she came, one day, upon Lavaine exercising his horse in a field, and by him she was taken to Sir Launcelot. Then, indeed, her heart was filled with grief when she saw the good knight to whom she had given her crimson sleeve thus laid low; so she abode in the hermitage, waiting upon Sir Launcelot and doing all within her power to lessen his pain.

After many weeks, by the good care of the hermit and the fair Elaine, Sir Launcelot was so far recovered that he might bear the weight of his armour and mount his horse again. Then, one morn, they left the hermitage and rode all three, the Fair Maid, Sir Launcelot, and Sir Lavaine, to the castle of Astolat, where there was much joy of their coming. After brief sojourn, Sir Launcelot desired to ride to court, for he knew there would be much sorrow among his kinsmen for his long absence. But when he would take his departure, Elaine cried aloud: "Ah! my lord, suffer me to go with you, for I may not bear to lose you." "Fair child," answered Sir Launcelot gently, "that may not be. But in the days to come, when ye shall love and wed some good knight, for your sake I will bestow upon him broad lands and great riches; and at all times will I hold me ready to serve you as a true knight may." Thus spoke Sir Launcelot, but the fair Elaine answered never a word.

So Sir Launcelot rode to London where the whole court was glad of his coming; but from the day of his departure, the Fair Maid drooped and pined until, when ten days were passed, she felt that her end was at hand. So she sent for her father and two brothers, to whom she said gently: "Dear father and brethren, I must now leave you." Bitterly they wept, but she comforted them all she might, and presently desired of her father a boon. "Ye shall have what ye will," said the old lord; for he hoped that she might yet recover. Then first she required her brother, Sir Tirre, to write a letter, word for word as she said it; and when it was written, she turned to her father and said: "Kind father, I desire that, when I am dead, I may be arrayed in my fairest raiment, and placed on a bier; and let the bier be set within a barge, with one to steer it until I be come to London. Then, perchance, Sir Launcelot will come and look upon me with kindness." So she died, and all was done as she desired; for they set her, looking as fair as a lily, in a barge all hung with black, and an old dumb man went with her as helmsman.

Slowly the barge floated down the river until it had come to Westminster; and as it passed under the palace walls, it chanced that King Arthur and Queen Guenevere looked forth from a window. Marvelling much at the strange sight, together they went forth to the quay, followed by many of the knights. Then the King espied the letter clasped in the dead maiden's hand, and drew it forth gently and broke the seal. And thus the letter ran: "Most noble Knight, Sir Launcelot, I, that men called the Fair Maid of Astolat, am come hither to crave burial at thy hands for the sake of the unrequited love I gave thee. As thou art peerless knight, pray for my soul."

Then the King bade fetch Sir Launcelot, and when he was come, he showed him the letter. And Sir Launcelot, gazing on the dead maiden, was filled with sorrow. "My lord Arthur," he said, "for the death of this dear child I shall grieve my life long. Gentle she was and loving, and much was I beholden to her; but what she desired I could not give." "Yet her request now thou wilt grant, I know," said the King; "for ever thou art kind and courteous to all." "It is my desire," answered Sir Launcelot.

So the Maid of Astolat was buried in the presence of the King and Queen and of the fellowship of the Round Table, and of many a gentle lady who wept, that time, the fair child's fate. Over her grave was raised a tomb of white marble, and on it was sculptured the shield of Sir Launcelot; for, when he had heard her whole story, it was the King's will that she that in life had guarded the shield of his noblest knight, should keep it also in death.

BOOK X
QUEEN GUENEVERE

CHAPTER XXXI
HOW MORDRED PLOTTED
AGAINST SIR LAUNCELOT

Before Merlin passed from the world of men, imprisoned in the great stone by the evil arts of Vivien, he had uttered many marvellous prophecies, and one that boded ill to King Arthur; for he foretold that, in the days to come, a son of Arthur's sister should stir up bitter war against the King, and at last a great battle should be fought in the West, when many a brave knight should find his doom.

Now, among the nephews of Arthur, was one most dishonourable; his name was Mordred. No knightly deed had he ever done, and he hated to hear the good report of others because he himself was a coward and envious. But of all the Round Table there was none that Mordred hated more than Sir Launcelot du Lac, whom all true knights held in most honour; and not the less did Mordred hate Launcelot that he was the knight whom Queen Guenevere had in most esteem. So, at last, his jealous rage passing all bounds, he spoke evil of the Queen and of Launcelot, saying that they were traitors to the King. Now Sir Gawain and Sir Gareth, Mordred's brothers, refused to give ear to these slanders, holding that Sir Launcelot, in his knightly service of the Queen, did honour to King Arthur also; but by ill-fortune another brother, Sir Agravaine, had ill-will to the Queen, and professed to believe Mordred's evil tales. So the two went to King Arthur with their ill stories.

Now when Arthur had heard them, he was wroth; for never would he lightly believe evil of any, and Sir Launcelot was the knight whom he loved above all others. Sternly then he bade them begone and come no more to him with unproven tales against any, and, least of all, against Sir Launcelot and their lady, the Queen.

The two departed, but in their hearts was hatred against Launcelot and the Queen, more bitter than ever for the rebuke they had called down upon themselves; and they resolved, from that time forth, diligently to watch if, perchance, they might find aught to turn to evil account against Sir Launcelot.

Not long after, it seemed to them that the occasion had come. For King Arthur having ridden forth to hunt far from Carlisle, where he then held court, the Queen sent for Sir Launcelot to speak with him in her bower. Then Agravaine and Mordred got together twelve knights, friends of Sir Gawain, their brother, and persuaded them to come with them for they should do the King a service. So with the twelve knights they watched and waited in a little room until they saw Sir Launcelot, all unarmed, pass into the Queen's chamber; and when the door was closed upon him, they came forth, and Sir Agravaine and Sir Mordred thundered on the door, crying so that all the court might hear: "Thou traitor, Sir Launcelot, come forth from the Queen's chamber. Come forth, for thy treason against the King is known to all!"

Then Sir Launcelot and the Queen were amazed and filled with shame that such a clamour should be raised where the Queen was. While they waited and listened in dismay, Sir Mordred and Sir Agravaine took up the cry again, the twelve knights echoing it: "Traitor Launcelot, come forth and meet thy doom; for thy last hour is come." Then Sir Launcelot, wroth more for the Queen than for himself, exclaimed: "This shameful cry will kill me; better death than such dishonour. Lady, as I have ever been your true knight, since the day when my lord, King Arthur, knighted me, pray for me if now I meet my death." Then he went to the door and cried to those without: "Fair lords, cease this outcry. I will open the door, and then ye shall do with me as ye will." With the word, he set open the door, but only by so much that one knight could enter at a time. So a certain Sir Colgrevance of Gore, a knight of great stature, pushed into the room and thrust at Sir Launcelot with all his might; but Sir Launcelot, with the arm round which he had wrapped his cloak, turned aside the sword and, with his bare hand, dealt Colgrevance such a blow on the helmet that he fell grovelling to the earth. Then Sir Launcelot thrust to and barred the door, and stripping the fallen knight of his armour, armed himself in haste with the aid of the Queen and her ladies.

All this while, Sir Agravaine and Sir Mordred continued their outcry; so when he was armed, Sir Launcelot called to them to cease their vile cries and the next day he would meet any or all of them in arms and knightly disprove their vile slander. Now there was not one among those knights who dared meet Sir Launcelot in the open field, so they were resolved to slay him while they had the advantage over him. When Sir Launcelot understood their evil purpose, he set wide the door and rushed upon them. At the first blow he slew Sir Agravaine, and soon eleven other knights lay cold on the earth beside him. Only Mordred escaped, for he fled with all his might; but, even so, he was sore wounded.

Then Sir Launcelot spoke to the Queen. "Madam," said he, "here may I no longer stay, for many a foe have I made me this night. And when I am gone, I know not what evil may be spoken of you for this night's work. I pray you, then, suffer me to lead you to a place of safety." "Ye shall run no more risk for my sake," said the Queen; "only go hence in haste before more harm befall you. But as for me, here I abide. I will flee for no traitor's outcry."

So Sir Launcelot, seeing that at that time there was naught he might do for Queen Guenevere, withdrew with all his kin to a little distance from Carlisle, and awaited what should befall.

CHAPTER XXXII
THE TRIAL OF THE QUEEN

When Mordred escaped Sir Launcelot, he got to horse, all wounded as he was, and never drew rein till he had found King Arthur, to whom he told all that had happened.

Then great was the King's grief. Despite all that Mordred could say, he was slow to doubt Sir Launcelot, whom he loved, but his mind was filled with forebodings; for many a knight had been slain, and well he knew that their kin would seek vengeance on Sir Launcelot, and the noble fellowship of the Round Table be utterly destroyed by their feuds.

All too soon, it proved even as the King had feared. Many were found to hold with Sir Mordred; some because they were kin to the knights that had been slain, some from envy of the honour and worship of the noble Sir Launcelot; and among them even were those who dared to raise their voice against the Queen herself, calling for judgment upon her as leagued with a traitor against the King, and as having caused the death of so many good knights. Now in those days the law was that if any one were accused of treason by witnesses, or taken in the act, that one should die the death by burning, be it man or woman, knight or churl. So then the murmurs grew to a loud clamour that the law should have its course, and that King Arthur should pass sentence on the Queen. Then was the King's woe doubled; "For," said he, "I sit as King to be a rightful judge and keep all the law; wherefore I may not do battle for my own Queen, and now there is none other to help her." So a decree was issued that Queen Guenevere should be burnt at the stake outside the walls of Carlisle.

Forthwith, King Arthur sent for his nephew, Sir Gawain, and said to him: "Fair nephew, I give it in charge to you to see that all is done as has been decreed." But Sir Gawain answered boldly: "Sir King, never will I be present to see my lady the Queen die. It is of ill counsel that ye have consented to her death." Then the King bade Gawain send his two young brothers, Sir Gareth and Sir Gaheris, to receive his commands, and these he desired to attend the Queen to the place of execution. So Gareth made answer for both: "My Lord the King, we owe you obedience in all things, but know that it is sore against our wills that we obey you in this; nor will we appear in arms in the place where that noble lady shall die"; then sorrowfully they mounted their horses, and rode to Carlisle.

When the day appointed had come, the Queen was led forth to a place without the walls of Carlisle, and there she was bound to the stake to be burnt to death. Loud were her ladies' lamentations, and many a lord was found to weep at that grievous sight of a Queen brought so low; yet was there none who dared come forward as her champion, lest he should be suspected of treason. As for Gareth and Gaheris, they could not bear the sight and stood with their faces covered in their mantles. Then, just as the torch was to be applied to the faggots, there was a sound as of many horses galloping, and the next instant a band of knights rushed upon the astonished throng, their leader cutting down all who crossed his path until he had reached the Queen, whom he lifted to his saddle and bore from the press. Then all men knew that it was Sir Launcelot, come knightly to rescue the Queen, and in their hearts they rejoiced. So with little hindrance they rode away, Sir Launcelot and all his kin with the Queen in their midst, till they came to the castle of the Joyous Garde where they held the Queen in safety and all reverence.

But of that day came a kingdom's ruin, for among the slain were Gawain's brothers, Sir Gareth and Sir Gaheris. Now Sir Launcelot loved Sir Gareth as if he had been his own younger brother, and himself had knighted him; but, in the press, he struck at him and killed him, not seeing that he was unarmed and weaponless; and in like wise, Sir Gaheris met his death. So when word was brought to King Arthur of what had passed, Sir Gawain asked straightway how his brothers had fared. "Both are slain," said the messenger. "Alas! my dear brothers!" cried Sir Gawain; "how came they by their death?" "They were both slain by Sir Launcelot." "That will I never believe," cried Sir Gawain; "for my brother, Sir Gareth, had such love for Sir Launcelot that there was naught Sir Launcelot could ask him that he would not do." But the man said again: "He is slain, and by Sir Launcelot."

Then, from sheer grief, Sir Gawain fell swooning to the ground. When he was recovered, he said: "My Lord and uncle, is it even as this man says, that Sir Launcelot has slain my brother Sir Gareth?" "Alas!" said the King, "Launcelot rode upon him in the press and slew him, not seeing who he was or that he was unarmed." "Then," cried Gawain fiercely, "here I make my avow. Never, while my life lasts, will I leave Sir Launcelot in peace until he has rendered me account for the slaying of my brother." From that day forth, Sir Gawain would not suffer the King to rest until he had gathered all his host and marched against the Joyous Garde. Thus began the war which broke up the fellowship of the Round Table.

CHAPTER XXXIII
HOW SIR GAWAIN DEFIED
SIR LAUNCELOT

Now it came to the ears of the Pope in Rome that King Arthur was besieging Sir Launcelot in his castle of the Joyous Garde, and it grieved him that there should be strife between two such goodly knights, the like of whom was not to be found in Christendom. So he called to him the Bishop of Rochester, and bade him carry word to Britain, both to Arthur and to Sir Launcelot, that they should be reconciled, the one to the other, and that King Arthur should receive again Queen Guenevere.

Forthwith Sir Launcelot desired of King Arthur assurance of liberty and reverence for the Queen, as also safe conduct for himself and his knights, that he might bring Dame Guenevere, with due honour, to the King at Carlisle; and thereto the King pledged his word.

So Launcelot set forth with the Queen, and behind them rode a hundred knights arrayed in green velvet, the housings of the horses of the same all studded with precious stones; thus they passed through the city of Carlisle, openly, in the sight of all, and there were many who rejoiced that the Queen was come again and Sir Launcelot with her, though they of Gawain's party scowled upon him.

When they were come into the great hall where Arthur sat, with Sir Gawain and other great lords about him, Sir Launcelot led Guenevere to the throne and both knelt before the King; then, rising, Sir Launcelot lifted the Queen to her feet, and thus he spoke to King Arthur, boldly and well before the whole court: "My lord, Sir Arthur, I bring you here your Queen, than whom no truer nor nobler lady ever lived; and here stand I, Sir Launcelot du Lac, ready to do battle with any that dare gainsay it"; and with these words Sir Launcelot turned and looked upon the lords and knights present in their places, but none would challenge him in that cause, not even Sir Gawain, for he had ever affirmed that Dame Guenevere was a true and honourable lady.

Then Sir Launcelot spoke again: "Now, my Lord Arthur, in my own defence it behoves me to say that never in aught have I been false to you. That I slew certain knights is true; but I hold me guiltless, seeing that they brought death upon themselves. For no sooner had I gone to the Queen's bower, as she had commanded me, than they beset the door, with shameful outcry, that all the court might hear, calling me traitor and felon knight." "And rightly they called you," cried Sir Gawain fiercely. "My lord, Sir Gawain," answered Sir Launcelot, "in their quarrel they proved not themselves right, else had not I, alone, encountered fourteen knights and come forth unscathed."

Then said King Arthur: "Sir Launcelot, I have ever loved you above all other knights, and trusted you to the uttermost; but ill have ye done by me and mine." "My lord," said Launcelot, "that I slew Sir Gareth I shall mourn as long as life lasts. As soon would I have slain my own nephew, Sir Bors, as have harmed Sir Gareth wittingly; for I myself made him knight, and loved him as my brother." "Liar and traitor," cried Sir Gawain, "ye slew him, defenceless and unarmed." "It is full plain, Sir Gawain," said Launcelot, "that never again shall I have your love; and yet there has been old kindness between us, and once ye thanked me that I saved your life." "It shall not avail you now," said Sir Gawain; "traitor ye are, both to the King and to me. Know that, while life lasts, never will I rest until I have avenged my brother Sir Gareth's death upon you." "Fair nephew," said the King, "cease your brawling. Sir Launcelot has come under surety of my word that none shall do him harm. Elsewhere, and at another time, fasten a quarrel upon him, if quarrel ye must." "I care not," cried Sir Gawain fiercely. "The proud traitor trusts so in his own strength that he thinks none dare meet him. But here I defy him and swear that, be it in open combat or by stealth, I shall have his life. And know, mine uncle and King, if I shall not have your aid, I and mine will leave you for ever, and, if need be, fight even against you." "Peace," said the King; and to Sir Launcelot: "We give you fifteen days in which to leave this kingdom." Then Sir Launcelot sighed heavily and said: "Full well I see that no sorrow of mine for what is past availeth me." Then he went to the Queen where she sat, and said: "Madam, the time is come when I must leave this fair realm that I have loved. Think well of me, I pray you, and send for me if ever there be aught in which a true knight may serve lady." Therewith he turned him about and, without greeting to any, passed through the hall, and with his faithful knights rode to the Joyous Garde, though ever thereafter, in memory of that sad day, he called it the Dolorous Garde.

There he called about him his friends and kinsmen, saying: "Fair Knights, I must now pass into my own lands." Then they all, with one voice, cried that they would go with him. So he thanked them, promising them all fair estates and great honour when they were come to his kingdom; for all France belonged to Sir Launcelot. Yet was he loth to leave the land where he had followed so many glorious adventures, and sore he mourned to part in anger from King Arthur. "My mind misgives me," said Sir Launcelot, "but that trouble shall come of Sir Mordred, for he is envious and a mischief-maker, and it grieves me that never more I may serve Sir Arthur and his realm."

So Sir Launcelot sorrowed; but his kinsmen were wroth for the dishonour done him, and making haste to depart, by the fifteenth day they were all embarked to sail overseas to France.

CHAPTER XXXIV
HOW KING ARTHUR AND SIR GAWAIN WENT TO FRANCE

From the day when Sir Launcelot brought the Queen to Carlisle, never would Gawain suffer the King to be at rest; but always he desired him to call his army together that they might go to attack Sir Launcelot in his own land.

Now King Arthur was loth to war against Sir Launcelot; and seeing this, Sir Gawain upbraided him bitterly. "I see well it is naught to you that my brother, Sir Gareth, died fulfilling your behest. Little ye care if all your knights be slain, if only the traitor Launcelot escape. Since, then, ye will not do me justice nor avenge your own nephew, I and my fellows will take the traitor when and how we may. He trusts in his own might that none can encounter with him; let see if we may not entrap him."

Thus urged, King Arthur called his army together and bade collect a great fleet; for rather would he fight openly with Sir Launcelot than that Sir Gawain should bring such dishonour upon himself as to slay a noble knight treacherously. So with a great host, the King passed overseas to France, leaving Sir Mordred to rule Britain in his stead.

When Launcelot heard that King Arthur and Sir Gawain were coming against him, he withdrew into the strong castle of Benwick; for unwilling indeed was he to fight with the King, or to do an injury to Sir Gareth's brother. The army passed through the land, laying it waste, and presently encamped about the castle, laying close siege to it; but so thick were the walls, and so watchful the garrison, that in no way could they prevail against it.

One day, there came to Sir Launcelot seven brethren, brave knights of Wales, who had joined their fortunes to his, and said: "Sir Launcelot, bid us sally forth against this host which has invaded and laid waste your lands, and we will scatter it; for we are not wont to cower behind walls." "Fair lords," answered Launcelot, "it is grief to me to war on good Christian knights, and especially on my lord, King Arthur. Have but patience and I will send to him and see if, even now, there may not be a treaty of peace between us; for better far is peace than war." So Sir Launcelot sought out a damsel and, mounting her upon a palfrey, bade her ride to King Arthur's camp and require of the King to cease warring on his lands, proffering fair terms of peace. When the damsel came to the camp, there met her Sir Lucan the Butler, "Fair damsel," said Sir Lucan, "do ye come from Sir Launcelot?" "Yea, in good truth," said the damsel; "and, I pray you, lead me to King Arthur." "Now, may ye prosper in your errand," said Sir Lucan. "Our King loves Sir Launcelot dearly and wishes him well; but Sir Gawain will not suffer him to be reconciled to him." So when the damsel had come before the King, she told him all her tale, and much she said of Sir Launcelot's love and good-will to his lord the King, so that the tears stood in Arthur's eyes. But Sir Gawain broke in roughly: "My Lord and uncle, shall it be said of us that we came hither with such a host to hie us home again, nothing done, to be the scoff of all men?" "Nephew," said the King, "methinks Sir Launcelot offers fair and generously. It were well if ye would accept his proffer. Nevertheless, as the quarrel is yours, so shall the answer be." "Then, damsel," said Sir Gawain, "say unto Sir Launcelot that the time for peace is past. And tell him that I, Sir Gawain, swear by the faith I owe to knighthood that never will I forego my revenge."

So the damsel returned to Sir Launcelot and told him all. Sir Launcelot's heart was filled with grief nigh unto breaking; but his knights were enraged and clamoured that he had endured too much of insult and wrong, and that he should lead them forth to battle. Sir Launcelot armed him sorrowfully, and presently the gates were set open and he rode forth, he and all his company. But to all his knights he had given commandment that none should seek King Arthur; "For never," said he, "will I see the noble King, who made me knight, either killed or shamed."

Fierce was the battle between those two hosts. On Launcelot's side, Sir Bors and Sir Lavaine and many another did right well; while on the other side, King Arthur bore him as the noble knight he was, and Sir Gawain raged through the battle, seeking to come at Sir Launcelot. Presently, Sir Bors encountered with King Arthur, and unhorsed him. This Sir Launcelot saw and, coming to the King's side, he alighted and, raising him from the ground, mounted him upon his own horse. Then King Arthur, looking upon Launcelot, cried: "Ah! Launcelot, Launcelot! That ever there should be war between us two!" and tears stood in the King's eyes. "Ah! my Lord Arthur," cried Sir Launcelot, "I pray you stay this war." As they spoke thus, Sir Gawain came upon them, and, miscalling Sir Launcelot traitor and coward, had almost ridden upon him before Launcelot could provide him of another horse. Then the two hosts drew back, each on its own side, to see the battle between Sir Launcelot and Sir Gawain; for they wheeled their horses, and departing far asunder, rushed again upon each other with the noise of thunder, and each bore the other from his horse. Then they put their shields before them and set on each other with their swords; but while ever Sir Gawain smote fiercely, Sir Launcelot was content only to ward off blows, because he would not, for Sir Gareth's sake, do any harm to Sir Gawain. But the more Sir Launcelot forbore him, the more furiously Sir Gawain struck, so that Sir Launcelot had much ado to defend himself, and at the last smote Gawain on the helm so mightily that he bore him to the ground. Then Sir Launcelot stood back from Sir Gawain. But Gawain cried: "Why do ye draw back, traitor knight? Slay me while ye may, for never will I cease to be your enemy while my life lasts." "Sir," said Launcelot, "I shall withstand you as I may; but never will I smite a fallen knight." Then he spoke to King Arthur: "My Lord, I pray you, if but for this day, draw off your men. And think upon our former love if ye may; but, be ye friend or foe, God keep you." Thereupon Sir Launcelot drew off with his men into his castle, and King Arthur and his company to their tents. As for Sir Gawain, his squires bore him to his tent where his wounds were dressed.

BOOK XI
THE MORTE D'ARTHUR

CHAPTER XXXV
MORDRED THE TRAITOR

So Sir Gawain lay healing of the grim wound which Sir Launcelot had given him, and there was peace between the two armies, when there came messengers from Britain bearing letters for King Arthur; and more evil news than they brought might not well be, for they told how Sir Mordred had usurped his uncle's realm. First, he had caused it to be noised abroad that King Arthur was slain in battle with Sir Launcelot, and, since there be many ever ready to believe any idle rumour and eager for any change, it had been no hard task for Sir Mordred to call the lords to a Parliament and persuade them to make him king. But the Queen could not be brought to believe that her lord was dead, so she took refuge in the Tower of London from Sir Mordred's violence, nor was she to be induced to leave her strong refuge for aught that Mordred could promise or threaten.

This was the news that came to Arthur as he lay encamped about Sir Launcelot's castle of Benwick. Forthwith he bade his host make ready to move, and when they had reached the coast, they embarked and made sail to reach Britain with all possible speed.

Sir Mordred, on his part, had heard of their sailing, and hasted to get together a great army. It was grievous to see how many a stout knight held by Mordred, ay, even many whom Arthur himself had raised to honour and fortune; for it is the nature of men to be fickle. Thus it was that, when Arthur drew near to Dover, he found Mordred with a mighty host, waiting to oppose his landing. Then there was a great sea-fight, those of Mordred's party going out in boats, great and small, to board King Arthur's ships and slay him and his men or ever they should come to land. Right valiantly did King Arthur bear him, as was his wont, and boldly his followers fought in his cause, so that at last they drove off their enemies and landed at Dover in spite of Mordred and his array. For that time Mordred fled, and King Arthur bade those of his party bury the slain and tend the wounded.

So as they passed from ship to ship, salving and binding the hurts of the men, they came at last upon Sir Gawain, where he lay at the bottom of a boat, wounded to the death, for he had received a great blow on the wound that Sir Launcelot had given him. They bore him to his tent, and his uncle, the King, came to him, sorrowing beyond measure. "Methinks," said the King, "my joy on earth is done; for never have I loved any men as I have loved you, my nephew, and Sir Launcelot. Sir Launcelot I have lost, and now I see you on your death-bed." "My King," said Sir Gawain, "my hour is come, and I have got my death at Sir Launcelot's hand; for I am smitten on the wound he gave me. And rightly am I served, for of my willfulness and stubbornness comes this unhappy war. I pray you, my uncle, raise me in your arms and let me write to Sir Launcelot before I die."

Thus, then, Sir Gawain wrote: "To Sir Launcelot, the noblest of all knights, I, Gawain, send greeting before I die. For I am smitten on the wound ye gave me before your castle of Benwick in France, and I bid all men bear witness that I sought my own death and that ye are innocent of it. I pray you, by our friendship of old, come again into Britain, and when ye look upon my tomb, pray for Gawain of Orkney. Farewell."

So Sir Gawain died and was buried in the Chapel at Dover.

CHAPTER XXXVI
THE BATTLE IN THE WEST

The day after the battle at Dover, King Arthur and his host pursued Sir Mordred to Barham Down where again there was a great battle fought, with much slaughter on both sides; but, in the end, Arthur was victorious, and Mordred fled to Canterbury.

Now, by this time, many that Mordred had cheated by his lying reports, had drawn unto King Arthur, to whom at heart they had ever been loyal, knowing him for a true and noble king and hating themselves for having been deceived by such a false usurper as Sir Mordred. Then when he found that he was being deserted, Sir Mordred withdrew to the far West, for there men knew less of what had happened, and so he might still find some to believe in him and support him; and being without conscience, he even called to his aid the heathen hosts that his uncle, King Arthur, had driven from the land, in the good years when Launcelot was of the Round Table.

King Arthur followed ever after; for in his heart was bitter anger against the false nephew who had wrought woe upon him and all his realm. At the last, when Mordred could flee no further, the two hosts were drawn up near the shore of the great western sea; and it was the Feast of the Holy Trinity.

That night, as King Arthur slept, he thought that Sir Gawain stood before him, looking just as he did in life, and said to him: "My uncle and my King, God in his great love has suffered me to come unto you, to warn you that in no wise ye fight on the morrow; for if ye do, ye shall be slain, and with you the most part of the people on both sides. Make ye, therefore, treaty for a month, and within that time, Sir Launcelot shall come to you with all his knights, and ye shall overthrow the traitor and all that hold with him." Therewith, Sir Gawain vanished. Immediately, the King awoke and called to him the best and wisest of his knights, the two brethren, Sir Lucan the Butler and Sir Bedivere, and others, to whom he told his dream. Then all were agreed that, on any terms whatsoever, a treaty should be made with Sir Mordred, even as Sir Gawain had said; and, with the dawn, messengers went to the camp of the enemy, to call Sir Mordred to a conference. So it was determined that the meeting should take place in the sight of both armies, in an open space between the two camps, and that King Arthur and Mordred should each be accompanied by fourteen knights. Little enough faith had either in the other, so when they set forth to the meeting, they bade their hosts join battle if ever they saw a sword drawn. Thus they went to the conference.

Now as they talked, it befell that an adder, coming out of a bush hard by, stung a knight in the foot; and he, seeing the snake, drew his sword to kill it and thought no harm thereby. But on the instant that the sword flashed, the trumpets blared on both sides and the two hosts rushed to battle. Never was there fought a fight of such bitter enmity; for brother fought with brother, and comrade with comrade, and fiercely they cut and thrust, with many a bitter word between; while King Arthur himself, his heart hot within him, rode through and through the battle, seeking the traitor Mordred. So they fought all day, till at last the evening fell. Then Arthur, looking around him, saw of his valiant knights but two left, Sir Lucan and Sir Bedivere, and these sore wounded; and there, over against him, by a great heap of the dead, stood Sir Mordred, the cause of all this ruin. Thereupon the King, his heart nigh broken with grief for the loss of his true knights, cried with a loud voice: "Traitor! now is thy doom upon thee!" and with his spear gripped in both hands, he rushed upon Sir Mordred and smote him that the weapon stood out a fathom behind. And Sir Mordred knew that he had his death-wound. With all the might that he had, he thrust him up the spear to the haft and, with his sword, struck King Arthur upon the head, that the steel pierced the helmet and bit into the head; then he fell back, stark and dead.

Sir Lucan and Sir Bedivere went to the King where he lay, swooning from the blow, and bore him to a little chapel on the sea-shore. As they laid him on the ground, Sir Lucan fell dead beside the King, and Arthur, coming to himself, found but Sir Bedivere alive beside him.

CHAPTER XXXVII
THE PASSING OF ARTHUR

So King Arthur lay wounded to the death, grieving, not that his end was come, but for the desolation of his kingdom and the loss of his good knights. And looking upon the body of Sir Lucan, he sighed and said: "Alas! true knight, dead for my sake! If I lived, I should ever grieve for thy death, but now mine own end draws nigh." Then, turning to Sir Bedivere, who stood sorrowing beside him, he said: "Leave weeping now, for the time is short and much to do. Hereafter shalt thou weep if thou wilt. But take now my sword Excalibur, hasten to the water side, and fling it into the deep. Then, watch what happens and bring me word thereof." "My Lord," said Sir Bedivere, "your command shall be obeyed"; and taking the sword, he departed. But as he went on his way, he looked on the sword, how wondrously it was formed and the hilt all studded with precious stones; and, as he looked, he called to mind the marvel by which it had come into the King's keeping. For on a certain day, as Arthur walked on the shore of a great lake, there had appeared above the surface of the water a hand brandishing a sword. On the instant, the King had leaped into a boat, and, rowing into the lake, had got the sword and brought it back to land. Then he had seen how, on one side the blade, was written, "Keep me," but on the other, "Throw me away," and, sore perplexed, he had shown it to Merlin, the great wizard, who said: "Keep it now. The time for casting away has not yet come." Thinking on this, it seemed to Bedivere that no good, but harm, must come of obeying the King's word; so hiding the sword under a tree, he hastened back to the little chapel. Then said the King: "What saw'st thou?" "Sir," answered Bedivere, "I saw naught but the waves, heard naught but the wind." "That is untrue," said King Arthur; "I charge thee, as thou art true knight, go again and spare not to throw away the sword."

Sir Bedivere departed a second time, and his mind was to obey his lord; but when he took the sword in his hand, he thought: "Sin it is and shameful, to throw away so glorious a sword." Then, hiding it again, he hastened back to the King, "What saw'st thou?" said Sir Arthur. "Sir, I saw the water lap on the crags." Then spoke the King in great wrath: "Traitor and unkind! Twice hast thou betrayed me! Art dazzled by the splendour of the jewels, thou that, till now, hast ever been dear and true to me? Go yet again, but if thou fail me this time, I will arise and, with mine own hands, slay thee."

Then Sir Bedivere left the King and, that time, he took the sword quickly from the place where he had hidden it and, forbearing even to look upon it, he twisted the belt about it and flung it with all his force into the water. A wondrous sight he saw, for, as the sword touched the water, a hand rose from out the deep, caught it, brandished it thrice, and drew it beneath the surface.

Sir Bedivere hastened back to the King and told him what he had seen. "It is well," said Arthur; "now, bear me to the water's edge; and hasten, I pray thee, for I have tarried over-long and my wound has taken cold." So Sir Bedivere raised the King on his back and bore him tenderly to the lonely shore, where the lapping waves floated many an empty helmet and the fitful moonlight fell on the upturned faces of the dead. Scarce had they reached the shore when there hove in sight a barge, and on its deck stood three tall women, robed all in black and wearing crowns on their heads. "Place me in the barge," said the King, and softly Sir Bedivere lifted the King into it. And these three Queens wept sore over Arthur, and one took his head in her lap and chafed his hands, crying: "Alas! my brother, thou hast been over-long in coming and, I fear me, thy wound has taken cold." Then the barge began to move slowly from the land. When Sir Bedivere saw this, he lifted up his voice and cried with a bitter cry: "Ah! my Lord Arthur, thou art taken from me! And I, whither shall I go?" "Comfort thyself," said the King, "for in me is no comfort more. I pass to the Valley of Avilion, to heal me of my grievous wound. If thou seest me never again, pray for me."

So the barge floated away out of sight, and Sir Bedivere stood straining his eyes after it till it had vanished utterly. Then he turned him about and journeyed through the forest until, at daybreak, he reached a hermitage. Entering it, he prayed the holy hermit that he might abide with him, and there he spent the rest of his life in prayer and holy exercise.

But of King Arthur is no more known. Some men, indeed, say that he is not dead, but abides in the happy Valley of Avilion until such time as his country's need is sorest, when he shall come again and deliver it. Others say that, of a truth, he is dead, and that, in the far West, his tomb may be seen, and written on it these words:

"Here lies Arthur, once King and King to be."

CHAPTER XXXVIII
THE DEATH OF SIR LAUNCELOT
AND OF THE QUEEN

When news reached Sir Launcelot in his own land of the treason of Mordred, he gathered his lords and knights together, and rested not till he had come to Britain to aid King Arthur. He landed at Dover, and there the evil tidings were told him, how the King had met his death at the hands of his traitor nephew. Then was Sir Launcelot's heart nigh broken for grief. "Alas!" he cried, "that I should live to know my King overthrown by such a felon! What have I done that I should have caused the deaths of the good knights, Sir Gareth, Sir Gaheris, and Sir Gawain, and yet that such a villain should escape my sword!" Then he desired to be led to Sir Gawain's tomb where he remained long in prayer and in great lamentation; after which he called to him his kinsmen and friends, and said to them: "My fair lords, I thank you all most heartily that, of your courtesy, ye came with me to this land. That we be come too late is a misfortune that might not be avoided, though I shall mourn it my life long. And now I will ride forth alone to find my lady the Queen in the West, whither men say she has fled. Wait for me, I pray you, for fifteen days, and then, if ye hear naught of me, return to your own lands." So Sir Launcelot rode forth alone, nor would he suffer any to follow him, despite their prayers and entreaties.

Thus he rode some seven or eight days until, at the last, he came to a nunnery where he saw in the cloister many nuns waiting on a fair lady; none other, indeed, than Queen Guenevere herself. And she, looking up, saw Sir Launcelot, and at the sight, grew so pale that her ladies feared for her; but she recovered, and bade them go and bring Sir Launcelot to her presence. When he was come, she said to him: "Sir Launcelot, glad am I to see thee once again that I may bid thee farewell; for in this world shall we never meet again." "Sweet Madam," answered Sir Launcelot, "I was minded, with your leave, to bear you to my own country, where I doubt not but I should guard you well and safely from your enemies." "Nay, Launcelot," said the Queen, "that may not be; I am resolved never to look upon the world again, but here to pass my life in prayer and in such good works as I may. But thou, do thou get back to thine own land and take a fair wife; and ye both shall ever have my prayers." "Madam," replied Sir Launcelot, "ye know well that shall never be. And since ye are resolved to lead a life of prayer, I, too, will forsake the world if I can find hermit to share his cell with me; for ever your will has been mine." Long and earnestly he looked upon her as he might never gaze enough; then, getting to horse, he rode slowly away.

Nor did they ever meet again in life. For Queen Guenevere abode in the great nunnery of Almesbury where Sir Launcelot had found her, and presently, for the holiness of her life, was made Abbess. But Sir Launcelot, after he had left her, rode on his way till he came to the cell where Sir Bedivere dwelt with the holy hermit; and when Sir Bedivere had told him all that had befallen, of the great battle in the West, and of the passing away of Arthur, Sir Launcelot flung down his arms and implored the holy hermit to let him remain there as the servant of God. So Sir Launcelot donned the serge gown and abode in the hermitage as the priest of God.

Presently there came riding that way the good Sir Bors, Launcelot's nephew; for, when Sir Launcelot returned not to Dover, Sir Bors and many another knight went forth in search of him. There, then, Sir Bors remained and, within a half-year, there joined themselves to these three many who in former days had been fellows of the Round Table; and the fame of their piety spread far and wide.

So six years passed and then, one night, Launcelot had a vision. It seemed to him that one said to him: "Launcelot, arise and go in haste to Almesbury. There shalt thou find Queen Guenevere dead, and it shall be for thee to bury her." Sir Launcelot arose at once and, calling his fellows to him, told them his dream. Immediately, with all haste, they set forth towards Almesbury and, arriving there the second day, found the Queen dead, as had been foretold in the vision. So with the state and ceremony befitting a great Queen, they buried her in the Abbey of Glastonbury, in that same church where, some say, King Arthur's tomb is to be found. Launcelot it was who performed the funeral rites and chanted the requiem; but when all was done, he pined away, growing weaker daily. So at the end of six weeks, he called to him his fellows, and bidding them all farewell, desired that his dead body should be conveyed to the Joyous Garde, there to be buried; for that in the church at Glastonbury he was not worthy to lie. And that same night he died, and was buried, as he had desired, in his own castle. So passed from the world the bold Sir Launcelot du Lac, bravest, most courteous, and most gentle of knights, whose peer the world has never seen ever shall.

After Sir Launcelot's death, Sir Bors and the pious knights, his companions, took their way to the Holy Land, and there they died in battle against the Turk.

So ends the story of King Arthur and his noble fellowship of the Round Table.